MEDIA
STUDIES

AN INTRODUCTION

Brian Dutton

Longman

For Susan

Thanks to Chris Keeble for the photgraphs on pages 145 and 149

Pearson Education Limited
Edinburgh Gate
Harlow
Essex
CM20 2JE
England and Associated Companies throughout the World

ISBN 0 582 40118 1

First published 1969

Third edition published 2000
Second impression 2001

Printed in Singapore (KHL)

Designed by Pumpkin House, Cambridge

The Publisher's policy is to use paper manufactured from sustainable forests.

CONTENTS

Source 1.1

WHAT ARE THE MEDIA?

Source 1.1

From Source 1.1 try to identify as many examples of the media as possible.

There is no precise or agreed definition of what to include or exclude as the main focus of media studies, but it is generally accepted that the following comprise the core areas:

- television and radio
- cinema
- newspapers and magazines
- advertising
- popular music
- the Internet

They all share an ability to reach large public audiences via the increasingly advanced technologies of print, video, sound, and so on.

WHY STUDY THE MEDIA?

Consider how large a part the media play in our daily lives. Here are three 'diaries' written by 16-year-old students describing how the media fit into a typical weekday.

ACTIVITIES

1 Write a similar diary for a typical weekday, describing the time you spend with the different media.
2 Try to calculate how many hours you spend in an average week:
   a watching television/videos;
   b listening to the radio;
   c reading magazines and newspapers;
   d listening to CDs and tapes;
   e using the Internet.

Most adults are unhappy about the amount of time young people spend with the media. In a recent survey of British children aged between 6 and 17 (*Young People New Media, 1999*), it was found that they spent 5 hours a day using different media. The survey went on to report that:

- two thirds have a television in their bedroom;
- most watch up to 2½ hours of television a day, compared to around 15 minutes reading books;
- nearly half have personal computers in the home;
- a third have TV linked games machines in their bedroom.

The survey concludes that books are being replaced by computers and the Internet as a source of information and by television as a source of narrative.

Marc – age 16

7.00am	Dad bursts into my room, opens the curtains and switches the TV on – it's Channel 4's *The Big Breakfast*.
7.30am	Actually get up, wash, dress and eat. Continue to watch *The Big Breakfast*. While the adverts are on, turn the radio onto Xfm.
8.00am	Rush out the door, making sure I have a copy of *Preacher* or *Q*.
8.20am	Talking with my friends about *Buffy the Vampire Slayer* and *The Simpsons*.
11.00am	Get my REM CD out and try to persuade my friends to give *New Adventures in Hi-fi* a listen.
4.30pm	Bus home. Depending who I sit next to, talk about comics, REM or movies.
5.15pm	Home! Time to watch the last 10-15 minutes of *Ricki Lake*.
6.00–7.00pm	Dinner while watching either *Hollyoaks* or the ITN news. Depends how good a mood Dad's in.
7.00pm	Collect e-mail and newsposts. Sit and read, reply to them and so on. Time for a quick computer game – *Final Fantasy VIII* or *Tomb Raider III*.
8.00pm	Usually either Buffy on video or a Kevin Smith film (*Clerks, Mallrats, Chasing Amy*).
9.00pm	If it's a Friday, I'll watch *Friends, South Park, Frasier* and *Amstrong and Miller*. If not I'll continue to watch the videos.
11.30pm	Music via earphones – REM.

Lisa – age 16

6.30am	Radio alarm goes off. Listen to Capital Radio until 6.50am.
6.50am	Go for a shower. Radio still playing in the background.
7.00am	Turn off radio. Turn on the TV to *The Big Breakfast* on Channel 4. Half watch the Johnny and Liza team while getting dressed, putting on my make-up and doing my hair.
7.30am	Go downstairs, watch more of *The Big Breakfast* and read *The Mirror*.
7.50am	Leave home for the bus stop.
8.00am	Bus leaves. Listen to Essex FM on bus radio.
8.30am	Get to college. Free morning period. Eat some breakfast in the canteen while listening to my Discman – *Fresh Hits 99*.
11.00am	Break. Sit about with some friends. Talk about last night's TV – *Neighbours, Let Them Eat Cake* and the brand new 'wide screen' *Blue Peter*.
12.00	Lunch. Read *J-17* magazine with a friend.
5.30pm	Dinner. Watched TV – *Byker Grove* and *Neighbours*.
6.00pm	Start doing Media homework while watching *Friends* and *Hollyoaks*.
7.00pm	English homework, listening to more *Fresh Hits*.
7.30pm	Settle down for a good night's TV.
	7.30 - *Eastenders*
	8.00 - watch video *St Elmo's Fire*
	9.30 - *Let Them Eat Cake*
	10.00 - *Soldiers to Be*
	10.30 - *Clive Anderson All Talk*
11.00pm	Retire to my room to watch half an hour of *The Stand* or read *The Green Mile* both by Stephen King.
11.30pm	Finally get some kip!

Gemma – age 16

7.00am	Mum wakes me up. Listen to Essex FM – Martin Day Breakfast Show – and get ready.
7.35am	Turn the radio off. Go downstairs and eat breakfast, watching *The Big Breakfast*, then later switch over to The Box and MTV.
8.00am	Leave the house and stop at the shops to buy the latest issue of *More*, plug in the earphones on my Walkman, and listen to the *Austin Powers* soundtrack on the way to the bus stop.
8.15am	Get on the bus and talk to a friend about what happened in *Hollyoaks* and *Eastenders* last night.
8.40am	Arrive at college, sit in the canteen, leafing through *More* and chatting to my mates.
12.00	Free block, read *More* from cover to cover.
5.10pm	Get home, watch the end of *Sister Sister*, then watch *Neighbours* while eating dinner.
6.15pm	Dad drives me to my boyfriend's – listen to Radio 1 in the car.
6.25pm	Arrive at my boyfriend's – watch *Emmerdale* and *Eastenders*, listen to Kiss *Smooth Grooves Summer 99* while he does his homework.
9.45pm	Get home, watch the rest of *Absolutely Fabulous*. Have a drink and then a shower.
10.00pm	Get ready for bed, pack my bag for college, then set the stereo to turn itself off in half an hour.
10.30pm	Drift off to sleep just as the stereo switches off my *Travis* CD.

The home has become the primary site of media consumption for most people ever since television became widely popular in the late 1950s.

Source 1.2a

Why is the activity 'Watching TV' (1.2a) not a very precise description of how people are using their television sets for entertainment or information?

ACTIVITY

Conduct a small survey of ten households to find out the following.
1 How many items from the table in source 1.2b are found in each household?
2 Who is most likely to use each item?
3 Is there any intention to buy or rent those items from the table not already acquired?

If television and other media – such as newspapers and radio – take up so much of our time, then it is important to ask why this is so.

Do the media shape the way we think? What do we learn about the world via the media?
Why are they so pleasurable for millions of people?
Who owns and controls the media?

These are some of the questions that make study of the media so important.

Source 1.2a

Participation[1] in home-based leisure activities in Great Britain, by gender		
	1977 %	1996–97 %
Males		
Watching TV	97	99
Visiting/entertaining friends or relations	89	95
Listening to radio	87	90
Listening to records/tapes/CDs	64	79
Reading books	52	58
DIY	51	58
Gardening	49	52
Dressmaking/needlework/knitting	2	3
Females		
Watching TV	97	99
Visiting/entertaining friends or relations	93	97
Listening to radio	87	87
Listening to records/tapes/CDs	60	77
Reading books	57	71
DIY	22	30
Gardening	35	45
Dressmaking/needlework/knitting	51	37

[1] Percentage of those aged 16 and over participating in each activity in the four weeks before interview.
Source: General Household Survey, Office for National Statistics

Home entertainment equipment in homes with children								
	1991 %	1992 %	1993 %	1994 %	1995 %	1996 %	1997 %	1998 %
Video recorder	87	91	90	94	93	96	94	92
Teletext	40	54	53	63	65	74	70	76
CD player	24	38	33	47	47	59	58	59
Video games	23	33	37	45	41	45	50	54
Computer	37	51	48	45	39	43	43	36
Satellite dish	11	14	17	19	20	23	24	26
Video camera	7	14	17	17	21	18	19	26
NICAM digital stereo television set	4	9	8	12	10	15	15	22
Cable television	4	4	3	10	9	10	15	17
Cable telephone	n/a	n/a	2	7	8	10	15	17
Widescreen television	n/a	n/a	n/a	7	6	5	5	7
Internet	n/a	n/a	n/a	n/a	n/a	4	7	10
Have none of these	7	5	5	2	2	1	2	1

Base: All TV viewers with children
Note: n/a = Not asked

Source 1.2b

THE CHANGING WORLD OF THE MEDIA

Source 1.3

1945

There was no television. About ten million households had a radio set and most were run off the mains, not off a battery. The compulsory annual licence fee cost ten shillings (50p). You had a choice of two BBC stations. One was 'serious'; the other broadcast light music and entertainment. The nine o'clock evening news had an audience of half the population during the war, but this fell quickly in 1945. The BBC had its own foreign correspondents but none yet for domestic news. Quite a lot of people listened to light music on Radio Luxembourg. You could also hear music at home on a wind-up gramophone with ten- or twelve-inch 78 rpm Bakelite records. These played for only a few minutes at a time.

Most people read one of nine London-edited, 'national' morning newspapers, delivered through the letter-box. If it was the Daily Mirror or Daily Sketch, it was tabloid. If not - and those papers had less than a quarter of the total circulation - it was broadsheet. Because of paper rationing it had only four to eight pages, unless it was The Times, which averaged nine. Most of the contents were news, not features. One person in five, mainly in the big cities, bought a locally published morning paper as well or instead. Local evening papers were smaller but more numerous (76 compared with 29). Londoners had a choice of three evening papers. Even more people read a Sunday paper than a daily, often for the sport. Nearly 750 towns had weekly papers.

The national dailies differed sharply in style between the low-circulation 'qualities' and the mass-circulation 'populars'. All nine were separately owned, mainly by elderly barons (barons in fact and in managerial style), such as Lord Beaverbrook and Lord Kemsley. They also owned Sunday papers.

On the news-stands, there were several popular illustrated weekly news and feature magazines: Everybody's, Illustrated, Picture Post. There were numerous general magazines and a growing market in women's weeklies and monthlies. Colour was limited. The brightest splash in the newsagent was probably the display of orange and green Penguin paperbacks - the main paperbacks available. 6,747 book titles were published. Boots and W.H. Smith ran cheap circulating libraries, supplementing the public libraries.

Regularly you went to the cinema. Thirty million cinema tickets a week were sold in 1945. The Times still listed cinemas as 'Picture Theatres'. The short weekly 'newsreels', a mixture of news and feature stories, gave a foretaste of TV news. Hollywood products dominated. In addition to the feature films, you saw a shorter, low-budget, 'B movie'. Films were censored for decency by Local Authorities, with the aid of an independent board.

In the press, 'taste' was largely a matter of editorial discretion. Four-letter words and topless girls were taboo. Tasteful, airbrushed nudes appeared in light monthly magazines such a Lilliput and Men Only.

Source 1.3 (C. Seymour-Ure, *The British Press and Broadcasting Since 1945*, Blackwell 1991)

THE MEDIA AND POPULAR CULTURE

It is clear from sources 1.2 a and b that the media play a significant part in most people's lives. Even if we would rather ignore or avoid the media, it would be virtually impossible to achieve. On any journey to work, school or the shops we are confronted with advertising posters on buses, hoardings and so on; newspaper headlines on street corners; music radio, tapes and CDs from passing cars. The media are almost inescapable. There are occasions when the broadcast media help to bring together a large proportion of the nation. Prior to television, radio achieved this – most notably during World War II. Since the Queen's Coronation in 1953, television has frequently been able to attract over 20 million viewers for a single programme. This might be for sport (such as England's World Cup matches), State occasions (such as Diana, Princess of Wales', funeral) and even for particular episodes of soap operas or sitcoms. Such events become national talking points and are lodged in popular consciousness. For instance, in a poll on television's greatest moments conducted by *The Observer* in 1999, the most memorable television moment was deemed to be man's landing on the moon in 1969. Other high-ranking moments inculded the World Cup Final (1966), the Live Aid Concert (1985), Diana, Princess of Wales', funeral (1997), *Only Fools and Horses* (when Del Boy falls through the bar,1989) and *Eastenders* (the divorce papers, Christmas 1986).

ACTIVITY

Compile a list of your own top 10 TV moments – those you have strongest memories of – and see if your choices are similar to those of friends or students in your class.

MAKING SENSE OF MEDIA CASE STUDY: LARA CROFT

Lara Croft is not a real person – she is a character from a computer game, Tomb Raider, who first appeared in 1996. How, then, might we begin to study or analyse Lara Croft as a media product?

Image

Source 1.4

What kind of female image is represented here?

Source 1.4

This is only one of hundreds of different images of Lara Croft circulating in the media. You may have other examples you could study that represent Lara Croft in alternative ways.

Unlike most famous female animated or cartoon characters, such as are found in many Disney firms, Lara Croft is an example of an *action heroine*. She is a character who takes risks and performs heroic deeds in order to triumph against the odds.

Sources 1.5a and b

1 Why do these two interpretations of Lara Croft differ so greatly?
2 What do you understand by the term 'icon'?
3 Who else might be considered a media or cultural icon?

Polly Vernon

Just another trashy male fantasy

Claims that cyber-heroine Lara Croft is a cultural icon are bogus

Lara Croft is the central character in the Tomb Raider series of PlayStation games. You might hear even more of Lara Croft, icon, over the next week or so, because Tomb Raider Four, Lara's latest romp through the darker side of archaeology, goes on sale mid-November. Lara Croft has taut thighs and a look of embryo/Barbie-gone-off-the-rails about her. Her ample proportions have sparked off more urban myths than a hall of residence full of bored students on soft drugs. Stumble upon a hidden password on level seven and she'll take her clothes off in a cave and gyrate naked to I Will Survive. Or maybe she won't. She's made the cover of The Face, toyed with a recording career, been interviewed extensively, modelled.

But she can't cut it for me. Personally, I like my icons to have a pulse. An element of free will. A sense of humour.

It bothers me that Lara Croft is considered an icon.

The truth is, unquestionably, real-life human women – even gorgeous ones – are too flawed to provide adequate stand-ins for a male-created, computer-generated thing.

The truth is that, if anything, Lara Croft is an anti-icon. Rather than being the devotional image of an original, significant, real person, she is an image that real people imitate. And that surely isn't a healthy state of affairs.

Source 1.5a (*The Guardian*, 8 November 1998)

Marketing

Lara Croft's image is so well known because she has appeared in so many different media-related products. *Lara Croft: The Movie* is the climax of many different appearances of Lara Croft's image that range from adorning the covers of countless games magazines to advertising Lucozade on television.

Of interest to media studies is the way a media image becomes a marketable product, capable of creating huge profits for the creators and distributors of the image. Eidos Interactive, the publisher of *Tomb Raider*, is the main company to gain from Lara Croft's success. Indeed, Eidos has gone to great lengths to 'control' Lara Croft's image by denying copyright to anyone who might in any way cause damage to her image. For example, Eidos went to court in America to prevent nude images of Lara Croft appearing in *Playboy* magazine (via a Lara Croft lookalike model).

> How do you describe a heroine? Courageous? Ingenious? Bold? Beautiful? Thrill-seeker? An adventurer?
> Lara Croft is all of these … and more. The subject of three of the most successful computer games of all time, she has captured the hearts of gamers worldwide. She is not real. But she could be. Maybe she does exist somewhere. If I could just find her …

Source 1.5b The Lara Croft Page (website)

Audience

There is little doubt that Lara Croft is one of the most popular computer/video games characters yet produced. Her appeal is global. This is helped by the fact that the games are played and understood easily across different cultures. Furthermore, because Lara Croft is a computerized image rather than a real person, this allows media audiences, especially games players, to project on to the character their own ideas of what she is like as a 'person'.

Source 1.6

1 How do you think the fact that games players can control what Lara Croft does affects their attitudes towards the character?
2 How might male and female games players, or audiences, respond differently in their interpretations of what Lara Croft represents?

Finally, it is important to note that Lara Croft has become what is referred to as a **cult** phenomenon. This means that she has developed a strong fan base whose interest has led them into acquiring additional information, images and possibly contact with other fans in order to share this enthusiasm. The development of the Internet has allowed such cult following (or subcultures) to flourish as never before.

Source 1.6

Source 1.7

Source 1.7

Identify another example of a media-based cult (for example, *The X-files*) and investigate the range of websites on the Internet devoted to the subject.

SUMMARY: THE SCHEME OF THIS BOOK

Key areas of study

1 *Language*
How do images, sounds and words create meaning in the media?

2 *Institutions*
What factors shape the production and circulation of media output such as television programmes, newspapers, films and so on?

3 *Representation*
How do the media make sense of the world?
What ideas, beliefs and attitudes are portrayed?

4 *Genre*
What are the distinctive styles and forms of media content?

5 *Audiences*
What are they and how do they make sense of the media?

These questions are not totally separate. In fact, many points crop up in more than one chapter. Like a jigsaw, each part of the picture only makes sense when fitted to another part.

Practical work

Throughout the book, the emphasis is on an active approach to media sutdies. Stimulus sources are provided for discussion, and practical activities suggested, which may be done individually or in groups.
Chapter 7 involves a full assessment of how to go about a practical media work, especially in relation to coursework assignments.

SEMIOLOGY

This is the study of the meaning of signs (sometimes called *semiotics*).

> **Source 2.1**
> What do these signs mean?

Although they may seem obvious to you, each sign has come to mean very different things to different people. The skull and crossbones has its roots in piracy, since when it has come to represent a warning against poison and, more recently, has been used in a TV

Source 2.1

Source 2.2

cartoon for children. The swastika in ancient times was used religiously to symbolize the power of God or nature. The German Nazi party adopted it in the 1930s, so that it became linked to fascist politics. Closer to today, youth groups such as hell's angels and punks have used it to decorate their clothes, while others have revived it as a signifier of their racial hatred of ethnic minorities in Britain. Such signs do not in themselves mean anything. People give them meaning, and it is the study of such meanings that is the purpose of semiology. A **sign** can be any physical form to which we give meaning, including words, pictures, colours, clothes, and so on. For example, the word 'bad' commonly means evil or wicked. However, in black American street culture, it has come to mean good (as used in the title of Michael Jackson's 1987 LP). The colour red might mean either Communism or danger.

ACTIVITY

1 Choose a colour and suggest what meaning(s) it has in our culture.
2 Choose a word that has more than one meaning (indicating that it has changed).

A sign such as a word or image is composed of two parts:

- the physical form – that which we can see or hear, called the **signifier**;
- the meaning of the form, which is the **signified** – for example, when we see a blue flashing light on top of a white car (two signifiers) we think it is a police car (what is signified).

Signs work together to create meaning.

ACTIVITY

List the signifiers that appear on cards to make us think it is Christmas time.

How much do they represent the real experience of Christmas?

Signs cannot be combined purely at random if they are to mean anything. They are combined according to certain rules, which form a **code**. For instance, traffic lights change colour in a standard sequence. Imagine the chaos if the red, amber and green lights switched at random! We learn to read signs according to codes (in the case of traffic lights, the highway code). Reading a book is no different. Words are combined according to the rules of spelling and grammar. When we read a sentence, we are **decoding** the meaning. All signs have to be decoded to be understood. While reading a book, you are decoding the meaning of the words in the text. In the media, not only books count as texts, but anything made of signs, such as photographs, TV programmes, adverts, records and magazines. A **text** is any collection of signs the meaning of which can be decoded.

Source 2.3

This is an advert for a car. What aspect of the car is being signified?

Source 2.3

THE NEW PEUGEOT 206 GTI
NOW YOU SEE IT. NOW YOU DON'T.

Source 2.4a Police using excessive force

Source 2.4b 'You're never alone with a Strand' (cigarette)

Source 2.4c

Number 10 in a range of 600 Jewson doors

IMAGES AND WORDS

Images and words are both examples of signs. An image by itself may have many 'different' meanings. An X can mean any of the following: wrong, crossroads or a kiss. The more uncertain the meaning of a sign, the more **open** it is. If an image is supplied with a written message, its meaning becomes more precise or **closed**. The words provide a reading or interpretation – they **anchor** the meaning of an image.

Source 2.4

How do the words 'anchor' the meaning of the pictures?

ACTIVITIES

1 Provide alternative interpretations for the pictures by writing a new caption for each one.
2 Collect four pictures from newspapers and magazines. Write a caption that represents each picture as:
   a an advert;
   b publicity for a film;
   c a news item.

Most images are open to a variety of interpretations. In semiology, when an image can mean different things to people, it is said to be **polysemic**. There may well be an intended or **preferred meaning** supplied by whoever has provided the media text, but the audience may not read the text in the same way. For example, for several years, the BBC portrayed Alf Garnett as a racist bigot in the comedy series *Till Death Us Do Part* and later in *In Sickness and Health* with the intention of making audiences laugh at him. However, it is clear that many viewers laughed *with* him, enjoying his prejudices, and thus reinforcing their own at the same time.

It may even be possible to change the meanings of media texts by adding your own message.

Source 2.5

1 How have the added messages changed the meanings of these adverts?
2 Why do you think this has been done?

Source 2.5

Television, radio, newspapers and other forms of the media use certain codes for creating meaning. These codes are based on rules and conventions, that have come to be recognized by audiences over time. A **convention** means a way of doing something that is generally accepted. In everyday life, we are surrounded by conventions, such as shaking hands when meeting someone or eating a meal with a knife and fork.

What are the codes and conventions associated with the different media?

Photography

A photograph appears to be a true record of life. The camera does not lie, but taking a picture does mean making choices, which can change the meaning of the picture. These include choosing the moment to take a shot and deciding what to include or leave out (this is called **framing** the picture). There are also choices regarding aspects like lighting, focusing, angle of view and whether to use black and white or colour film. The camera sees the world differently from human vision, as can be seen in the photographs on the next page.

Source 2.6 *Photographic codes*

Describe what you can see in each of the pictures. What is being drawn to our attention? Comment on the lighting, focusing, angle and framing in each picture.

Source 2.6

Newspaper codes

When reading newspapers it is possible to identify a variety of codes. All newspapers follow the rule that the most important story is presented on the front page near the top, usually accompanied by a picture. Even this rule has not always applied. The front page of *The Times* used to carry only classified adverts.

Source 2.7a (*The Sun*, 5 October 1999)

THE Sun

Tuesday, October 5, 1999   30p   THOUGHT: JOB BLOW

FREE SHOPPING AT TESCO
TOKEN 2 – SEE PAGE 23

FREE THE SIMPSONS VIDEO
TOKEN 4 – SEE PAGE 24

8 PAGE SIMPSONS PULLOUT INSIDE

Mile-High Mandy got randy on brandy

FIRST PIC OF JET GIRL

By GUY PATRICK and CAROLINE SIGLEY

THIS is Mandy Holt — the woman said to have performed a sex act on a stranger at 30,000ft.

And yesterday it was confirmed that free brandy she drank on the transatlantic flight tippled her over the top.

Passengers told how blonde Mandy, 36 – pictured yesterday – stripped to her bra and panties then joined the Mile-High Club with David Machin, 40.

Now their jobs could be on the line because of their antics in the business class section of

Continued on Page 12

David . . . romp on jet

EXCLUSIVE: HARRY ENFIELD ON HIS NEW MOVIE – PAGES 26 & 27

GREAT MINDS DON'T THINK ALIKE

Natasha Walter: So why is Cherie our new best friend?
'Why are the papers suddenly on Cherie Blair's side? Because they believe that, deep down, what every woman wants is to be a mother'
TUESDAY REVIEW, PAGE 11

Deborah Orr: In the land of idiots, Cliff Richard is king
'Worrying things are happening in my head. I am pleased that Sir Cliff has reached No 1; so pleased that I'm certain this is an important Pop Moment'
TUESDAY REVIEW, PAGE 5

THE TEMP IS BACK!
READ THE COLUMN THAT BECAME A BEST-SELLER
PAGE 8
PLUS
MEDIA
IN THE TUESDAY REVIEW

£15,000 TO BE WON
FOR YOUR CHRISTMAS SHOPPING SPREE
THIS SECTION
PAGE 23
TODAY COLUMN

THE INDEPENDENT

www.independent.co.uk

TUESDAY 30 NOVEMBER 1999 • No 4,093 • 45p (IR50p)

COLUMN ONE

'We gave thanks that our children escaped'

John Cobb, a journalist at *The Independent*, reflects on the attack that shook his parish

ANY HOPES that we, the people of St Andrew's parish, could put behind us the trauma of the attack on Sunday, when a man ran amok with a Samurai sword, were dashed before then yesterday.

At 6.30am, Brook Road, in Thornton Heath, south London, was dark save for the lights from the television camera crew vans...

A historic day for Ulster as old enemies form a new government

By DAVID McKITTRICK
Ireland Correspondent

ULSTER UNIONISTS and Irish republicans were brought together yesterday in an unprecedented coalition government intended to pave the way for a new post-Troubles era in Northern Ireland.

The representatives of traditions which for centuries have been at loggerheads, often grappling together in lethal confrontation, suddenly chose their representatives to serve in a new cross-community executive.

Martin McGuinness, of Sinn Fein, once the epitome of militant republicanism and a particular Unionist hate-figure, is to take charge of Northern Ireland's schools as Minister for Education...

Sinn Fein's president, Gerry Adams (centre), with his newly appointed ministers Bairbre de Brun and Martin McGuinness at Stormont yesterday *Peter Macdiarmid*

INSIDE

Republicans, nationalists and enough Unionists have found enough common ground to proclaim: this is it, the new majority is Northern Ireland, the new way ahead
DAVID McKITTRICK, PAGE 3

America mourns death of an adorable failure

By MARY DEJEVSKY
in Washington

THERE WAS weeping and wailing, and much gnashing of bamboo in Washington yesterday at the news that Hsing-Hsing, the once incontrovertibly positive result of the meeting between Richard Nixon and Mao Tse-tung, is no more.

At 28 years old, Hsing-Hsing, who had suffered from kidney disease...

Hsing-Hsing: 'A gift of friendship from China'

Figures expose Britain's worst fertility clinics

By CHERRY NORTON
Health Correspondent

WOMEN OVER 35 years old who need fertility treatment can, for the first time, choose clinics which will give them a better chance of having a baby.

Official figures, for the 75 or so extra fertilisation (IVF) clinics in Britain, released today but seen in advance by *The Independent*...

IN THIS SECTION: WEATHER 2, CROSSWORD 30.   IN THE TUESDAY REVIEW: LETTERS 2, LEADERS & COMMENT 3-5, RADIO & TV 17-18

Radio codes

Radio is an **auditory** medium – it depends entirely on sound. Much is left to the imagination of the listener. There is a range of auditory signifiers for creating meaning. These include:

Words
This is the obvious language of radio. Different types of speaker may be signified by the tone of voice or speed of delivery. For example, a rural accent may be used to represent simplicity or lack of sophistication. A French or Italian voice may signify romance and charm.

Sounds
Sound effects are often used to create atmosphere and signify the context, where things are happening. Crying seagulls suggest the seaside, twittering birds the countryside, and roaring traffic the city streets. The sound of approaching footsteps, followed by a creaking door, may create suspence. Sounds may be faded in and out to signify time passing.

Music
This may also create mood, as it does in film and television. Usually it is played for its own enjoyment or as a **jingle**, for linking or introducing programmes.

ACTIVITIES

1 Listen to 15 minutes of radio drama (such as the BBC's *The Archers*) and note:
a   your impressions of the characters from their voices and speech;
b   how sound effects are used to signify the setting and action.
2 Record two radio adverts and analyse how each of the auditory signifiers – speech, music and sound effects – contributes to the overall meaning of the advert.

Film and television codes

How can film or television be thought of as a language? Unlike written and spoken language, there are no strict rules for creating meaning in film and video. Pop music videos have shown that virtually any combination of images can be shown with the music.

However, there are certain codes of language in film-making that audiences have learned to read. Watching television may seem like looking through a 'window on the world' in which the screen simply reveals what is there, but the images have been carefully selected in order to create certain meanings. What is seen is just as much a construction or product as a book or magazine written by an author. As with photography, there are many choices of shot for filming a subject. What we see on film is normally a much narrower field of vision than our own, which is roughly 180°. Try stretching out your arms and look straight ahead. You should just be able to see your arms out of the corners of your eyes.

The camera is therefore selective. What kinds of choices are possible?

Shot distance
This affects what we can see and how closely involved we become with a subject.

Source 2.8

1 Select three of these shots, and explain why they are selected for use in film or television.
2 Long shots are used more often in films, while close shots are used more often in television. Why do you think this is so?

Lighting
This affects the mood and atmosphere of a scene.

Very long shot

Long shot

Medium long shot

Medium shot

Close shot   **Source 2.8**

Focus

If only part of a picture is in focus, it draws our attention to its importance. How sharp or soft the focus is may also have an effect. Look at the picture adverts on page 71. Why is the focusing softer for the feminine perfume?

Angle

Camera shots are often from eye-level angle. This helps to make the viewing seem more natural and life-like. High-angle shots tend to reduce the importance of a subject, whereas low-angle shots may increase the sense of power or authority of a subject. Low-angle shots are more often used in film than television.

Camera movement

Choices here include:

- pan   = moving the camera from side to side;
- tilt   = moving the camera up or down;
- zoom = changing the lens to move closer to, or further away from, a subject;
- track = moving the camera forwards or backwards, either on wheels or hand-held.

ACTIVITY

You can see these visual codes in most films and television programmes. From two minutes of recorded fictional television, describe the choice of shot distance, lighting, focus, angle and camera movement. Try to suggest reasons for the various choices.

Source 2.9

1 Where is the source of lighting in these two shots?
2 How does the lighting affect your interpretation of the pictures?

Source 2.9

Sound

Words anchor the meaning of images in film and television as well as photographs. These may be spoken by the subjects appearing in the film, or there may be a voice-over commentary. Music and sound effects also add meaning (see the earlier section on radio).

ACTIVITIES

1 Make a list of different musical styles that may be heard in films and on television. Describe how each style affects the meaning of the pictures.
2 Record a short extract of a television documentary that has voice-over commentary and/or music and sound effects. Write your own script that can be added to the pictures with or without music, and played back with the video recording to create new meanings for the pictures.
(NB: Some video recorders have an audio overdub facility, so you can record the new soundtrack directly on to the videotape, instead of simply turning off the existing soundtrack.)

Figure 2.1 A modern television control room

Editing

Editing involves deciding which shots to use. If the pictures are live, the director has to select the camera position to use at that moment. If it is a recorded programme, the choice will be what to include or leave out, and how the shots should be linked. Linking shots can be done in several ways.

- **Straight cut** Changing immediately from one shot to another (the most commonly used link).
- **Fade** Making the picture slowly appear or disappear (to represent the beginning or end of a sequence of shots).
- **Wipe** One image removes another.
- **Dissolve** One image slowly emerges to replace the existing image (so for a moment you can see both images).

In addition, there are **special effects**. These include freeze frame, slow motion, split screen (showing more than one picture at the same time), image overlay (placing one picture over another) and computer graphics. Many of these special effects may be seen in pop videos.

PURELY,
NATURALLY,
YOURS

BUXTON NATURAL MINERAL WATER

FOUND PURELY IN BRITAIN

*Carte Noire
un café nommé désir*

Source 2.10

Advertising codes

Adverts draw on several codes including photography and written language. Therefore, decoding adverts (interpreting their meanings) requires analysis of a range of signifiers – images, words, sounds, and so on.

Source 2.10

What qualities of the product are being signified by the images and words in each of the adverts?

ACTIVITY

Collect four adverts for a similar type of product – perfume, motor cars, or soft drinks, for example – and describe how the images and the words (the signifiers) supply meanings about each product. Remember that colour is often an important part of the coding.

Narrative

Shots are linked in film and television in order to tell a story. The process of producing a story is referred to as **narrative**. This can be subdivided into the:

- **theme** – what the story is about.
- **plot** – what happens.
- **discourse** or narration – how the story is told.

We think in terms of stories all the time. What happened today? What will happen next? These questions are posed in our everyday conversations or in our fantasies. They might be answered in our diaries or letters. For centuries, the novel and the song have been popular forms of narrative.

Narrative in pop songs

One the whole, pop songs are about expressing emotion, often reflecting on love and romance – first meetings, being in love, breaking up, painful memories and so on. Sometimes, borrowing from the folk music tradition, songs may tell a story or convey a social or political message. This is especially the case with rap music, which is a musical form used by mainly black artists to express their own particular cultural experience, often in terms of direct political action.

Source 2.11 *Always*

1 Who is telling the story?
2 Why is the chorus important?
3 How might the music and singing add to the storytelling?

ACTIVITY

1 From your own music collection, listen to ten songs and describe the main narrative themes.
2 Select ten music videos and examine whether the visual representation of the song's lyrics changes or reinforces their meaning.

ALWAYS (JON BON JOVI)

This Romeo is bleeding
But you can't see his blood
It's nothing but some feelings
That this old dog kicked up

It's raining since you left me
Now I'm drowing in the flood
You see I've been a fighter
But without you, I give up

Now, I can't sing a love song
Like the way it's meant to be
Well, I guess I'm not that good
    any more
But baby, that's just me

Chorus
Yeah, I will love you baby
    – always
And I'll be there forever and a day
    – always
I'll be there 'til the stars don't
    shine
'Til the heavens burst and the
    words don't rhyme
And I know when I die, you'll be
    on my mind
And I'll love you – always

Now your pictures that you left
    behind
Are just memories of a different
    life
Some that made us laugh, some
    that made us cry
One that made you have to say
    goodbye

What I'd give to run my fingers
    through your hair
To touch your lips, to hold you
    near
When you say your prayers
Try to understand, I've made
    mistakes,
I'm just a man

When he holds you close, when
    he pulls you near
When he says the words you've
    been needing to hear
I'll wish I was him 'cause those
    words are mine
To say to you 'til the end of time

Yeah, I will love you baby
    – always
And I'll be there forever and a day
    – always
If you told me to cry for you, I
    could
If you told me to die for you, I
    would
Take a look at my face
There's no price I won't pay
To say these words to you

Well, there ain't no luck in these
    loaded dice
But baby if you give me just one
    more try
We can pack up our old dreams
    and our old lives
We'll find a place where the sun
    still shines

Yeah, I will love you baby
    – always
And I'll be there forever and a day
    – always
I'll be there 'til the stars don't
    shine
'Til the heavens burst
And the words don't rhyme
And I know when I die, you'll be
    on my mind
And I'll love you – always

Source 2.11 (Bon Jovi, *Always*, Polygram 1994)

In narrative, much can be left to the imagination as to what has happened or will happen. This applies even to single images that freeze a moment in time.

Source 2.12

What do you think might have happened before and after this photograph was taken?

Source 2.12

Name: <u>Nadia Clarkson</u>
Age: <u>Seventeen</u>
Secret: <u>I slept with my teacher and got him the sack</u>

Source 2.13 *My Guy* 26 November 1994

Photostory narrative

Source 2.13

Write a set of captions that could go in the empty bubbles so that the sequence of pictures tells a story. Compare your version with others.

ACTIVITY

Look at further photostories from teenage magazines, then make a list of the main plots and how the stories are developed (for example, a problem arises and is eventually solved). Are there any similarities between the stories?

Building narrative in film and television

Time

Only with live coverage on television is real time shown. Even then, the real flow of events is often interrupted, as in sport, where **action replays** are used. In telling a story, editing enables jumps in time to be made. A simple cut may move the story on or possibly lead the viewer back in time (via a flashback). **Fade-outs** or **dissolves** could mean a longer period of time passing. In many Hollywood films, passing time was represented by calendar pages being ripped off or the hands of a clock moving round. The faster the cutting, the greater the opportunity to speed up the story.

Point of view

When watching a film or television programme, the viewer is placed in a particular position to see the events. A common starting point is the **establishing shot** (usually long shot), which sets the general scene. Closer shots place the viewer in a more personal relationship with the subjects, especially when they are seen at eye level. The viewer may then be drawn in to see the story from the point of view of the participants.

Source 2.14

Describe what kind of story is developing here. How is the narrative developed in each shot?

Source 2.14 Visual flow (Roland Lewis, *The Video Maker's Handbook*, Pan, 1987)

Dodge City Storyboard

1 LONG SHOT EXTERIOR MAIN STREET, DODGE CITY. WE SEE A HOT, DUSTY WESTERN STREET. TWO MEN FACE EACH OTHER. THEY ARE NOW SOME DISTANCE APART.

2 FULL SHOT SHERIFF JIM KINCAID. JIM IS WEARING A WHITE HAT. HE HAS A GRIM EXPRESSION ON HIS FACE, AND A SHINY 5-POINT STAR ON HIS LAPEL.

3 FULL SHOT EVIL RANCE DEVLIN.
COMING TOWARD THE SHERIFF IS EVIL RANCE DEVLIN DRESSED ALL IN BLACK. HE IS CARRYING SIX GUNS THAT ARE ALMOST IDENTICAL TO THOSE THE SHERIFF HAS. RANCE LOOKS TO HIS LEFT.

4 INSERT CLOSE UP A CLOCK FACE.
WE SEE IT'S HIGH NOON.

5 CLOSE UP - KINCAID'S FACE. HE IS ALSO LOOKING AT THE CLOCK. HE TURNS AND LOOKS THE OPPOSITE WAY AT HIS DEPUTY WHO HAS ENTERED THE FRAME AS THE CAMERA PULLS BACK SLIGHTLY.
DEPUTY It's time
SHERIFF I know
DEPUTY Sure you don't want some help?
SHERIFF This is my battle. I've got to face him alone

6 LONG SHOT MAIN STREET, DODGE CITY.
WE RETURN TO THE FIRST SHOT AS WE SEE THE MEN START TO STRIDE TOWARDS EACH OTHER.

7 TRACKING MEDIUM SHOT SHERIFF KINCAID.
THE CAMERA TRAVELS WITH THE SHERIFF AS HE STRIDES TOWARDS THE ENEMY.
SHERIFF This is it for you, Devlin. I'm taking care of you once and for all.

8 TRACKING MEDIUM SHOT EVIL RANCE DEVLIN.
FROM THE OTHER DIRECTION COMES RANCE DEVLIN WITH A SNARL ON HIS LIPS.
RANCE We'll just see about that Sheriff.

9 CLOSE UP - DEVLIN'S GUNS. WE SEE DEVLIN FINGURING HIS PEARL HANDLED REVOLVER.

Figure 2.2 (R. Hirschman and R. Proctor *How to Shoot Better Video*, Hal Leonard Books)

The storyboard

This is the visual illustration or picture guide to how a story develops. It is much like a cartoon comic strip, except there are added details of how the camera is to be used to help develop the story. Figure 2.2 is an example of a simple storyboard.

For further discussion on constructing storyboards see pages 150–151.

| ACTIVITIES |
1 Try to provide details of the camera shots used in source 2.14 as if creating a storyboard for a film. For example, shot 3 = a medium long shot panning or tracking left to right.
2 Produce a storyboard of up to 12 shots that helps to build suspense.

The audience interest is created by a desire to know how, and in what form, normality will be restored by the end of the story. The posing of a riddle or puzzle is referred to as a **narrative enigma**. In the case of cinema, this is first established in the marketing publicity for a film. In particular, film posters help to create an enigma that the audience is encouraged to solve (by going to see the film!)

Source 2.15

Identify the narrative enigma(s) posed in each of the film posters.

Key elements of narrative

In most narrative there are certain elements that can be found whatever the media form. First, there is the **setting**. This is the time and place in which the action occurs. Usually, this is fairly obvious from the clothing people wear, the way they speak, the physical environment, and so on. Sometimes, additional details may be supplied so the audience knows exactly where and when the narrative is set.

In cinema, this may be revealed by the title, such as *Titanic* and *2001 A Space Odyssey* (made in 1968); the opening establishing shot – of the American West, the Manhattan Skyline (New York), and even a voice-over or on-screen title to inform the audience of the time and place in which the film is set.

Characters are essential if audiences are to have any interest in how a narrative develops. Because most media texts do not have the time and space to develop complicated individual characters, usually they will conform to recognizable types (see the discussion of stereotyping on page 70). We often know what kind of characters to expect from the setting. For example, a war film is likely to include a daring and brave hero, a young 'innocent' anxious about war and so on, and the characterization will be helped by factors such as appearance, speech, body language and action. In the case of cinema, the casting of certain actors may provide further clues as to the kind of character being portrayed. For example, it would be surprising if Tom Hanks was anything other than the hero in a Hollywood film.

Heroes and villains form much of the basis of **conflict** which drives forward narrative. This might be straightforward good versus evil, as in James Bond films, or could be the triumph of law and order, as in television series like *The Bill*. Even non-fictional media narratives contain conflict. News and sports stories are often built around the idea of struggles and competition between opposing forces, although who is right/wrong or good/evil may not be so clear.

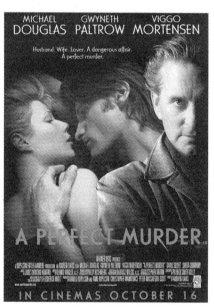

Source 2.15

When narratives are neatly ended or resolved and the audience is not left wondering what happens next, then these are referred to as being **closed**. Mainstream cinema is typically characterized by closed narrative (although there is a tendency to produce a sequel if the original film is very profitable).

ACTIVITY

Select three films with which you are familiar and identify the:

a setting;

b main characters and their role in developing the narrative;

c main form of conflict within the narrative;

d how the narrative is restored or closed

In comparison to cinema, television narrative has a tendency to be more **open-ended**. Serials are characterized by a continuous unfolding story over weeks, months or even years in the case of long-running soap operas of the likes of *Coronation Street* (which began in 1960). Where the narrative is dominated by one main story, then it is referred to as **single-strand narrative**, such as a murder mystery. If there are several stories running in parallel, as in a soap opera, then this is referred to as **multi-stranded narrative**.

Source 2.16

1 How many narrative enigmas relate to the character of Nina in EastEnders?

2 Examine an episode of EastEnders, or any other British soap opera, and list all the individual stories (or narrative strands). How many of these are beginning, developing or being resolved?

EastEnders

Blast from the past

A familiar face from Nina's former life threatens to reveal her secret...

Every soap character has a few skeletons in their closet and Queen Vic barmaid Nina Harris is no exception.

So far she has managed to keep her past life as a prostitute a secret from the residents of the Square, but the arrival this fortnight of Dean, a former client of hers, threatens to shatter the new life she has built up for herself.

"Dean turning up in Walford is Nina's worst nightmare come true," says Troy Titus-Adams, who plays her. "She never dreamt anyone would find out about her history and she is gutted that they now could."

So what does Dean want from Nina? "I can't say, but it's not very nice," sighs Troy. "He's definitely out to make trouble for her."

> "Dean is definitely out to make trouble for Nina"

Dean's arrival couldn't have come at a worse time. "Nina's just had a great night out with Grant when he appears," explains Troy. "The last thing she needs is him putting a spanner in the works."

So is a romance between Nina and Grant on the cards then? "Who knows?" says Troy. "People keep asking me, but I honestly don't know what's going to happen.

"That said, there is definitely something between Nina and Grant, but she's kept her distance recently because he has been kept busy with Courtney.

First, though, she's going to have to deal with Dean. Trouble is, who can she turn to for help? "There is a knight in shining armour who comes to her rescue," smiles Troy. "You will have to wait and see who it is, though."

Can Nina escape Dean's hold on her?

Source 2.16 (*Inside Soap*, 23 July 1999)

Realism

If you ever see old silent films, they often seem rather ridiculous, and certainly not realistic.

Questions for group discussion

1 Why do old films lack 'realism'?

2 What is meant by 'realism'?

3 Which television programmes seem most 'real' to you?

It may well be that your answer to the second question is something like 'true to life'. Modern television may seem more 'true to life' than old films because audience expectations have changed in line with technological developments such as colour, more sensitive cameras, deeper focus and so on. This implies that it is possible to achieve a pure reflection of reality, a true 'window on the world'.

However, television, film and even radio are only realistic in so far as we are not conscious that they have been put together by directors, producers and actors. Various techniques and conventions help to achieve this effect. In television drama, for example, locations or sets fit us into a 'real' world, the characters appear credible and every detail is made to seem authentic. The actors do not address the camera, for that would admit the existence of a separate audience.

The more involved the audience, the more 'real' the experience. Different types or genres of media output produce different kinds of realism, and as long as audiences recognize and accept each genre for what it is, such as a cartoon or a science fiction programme, then it can seem real within its own terms. For example, the cartoon characters *The Simpsons* are quite crude and unrealistic in terms of the way they are drawn. However, audiences find them so funny because their characters seem so real.

Often, it is only when conventions are broken, either accidentally (as shown on shows like *It'll Be Alright On The Night*) or deliberately (as in the spoof chat show *Knowing Me Knowing You*), that they are exposed as a construction.

Source 2.17

1 What narrative questions seem to be posed by each of the programmes described in the *Radio Times* extract?

2 Which programmes contain open-ended and which closed forms of narrative?

ACTIVITIES

1 How far do viewers think of soap characters and settings as real?

2 To what extent do soap operas represent reality? With reference to one soap opera, consider the following:

a the language spoken;
b the range of people represented – age groups, ethnic minorities and so on;
c the extent to which people know each other;
d the number of dramatic events;
e the relationship between the setting of the soap opera and the outside world, such as the worlds of work, leisure and national events.

Source 2.17

WEDNESDAY 12 January

TELEVISION

OTHER REGIONS

BBC1

8.00
Trude Mostue in Uganda where she is taking part in a project helping to stop the spread of disease from wild to domestic animals in **Vets in the Wild**

6.00 BBC News
PM with Huw Edwards, including weather summary

6.30 Regional news magazine
Followed by Weather with Sarah Wilmshurst

7.00 Big Break
Jim Davidson and John Virgo oversee another edition of the snooker-based game show. Tonight's players are Lee Richardson, Mark King and John Parrott.

7.30 Tomorrow's World
Tonight investigating a sound beam that could signal the end of noise pollution as it can only be heard by those in its path. Plus an experimental medical technique which could enable multiple sclerosis sufferers to renew their damaged immune systems. With Peter Snow, Philippa Forrester, Anya Sitaram, Jez Nelson, Lindsey Fallow and Nick Baker

8.00 Vets in the Wild
Continuing the twice-weekly series following Vets in Practice stars Trude Mostue and Steve Leonard on their adventure in the African bush. Tonight the pair find themselves in hospital following last week's road accident. They then fly on to Uganda to take part in a project to stop the spread of disease from wild animals to domestic animals.

8.30 Battersea Dogs' Home
Shauna Lowry works as a trainee van driver, collecting stray and abandoned dogs from police stations.

8.50 The National Lottery Third Degree
Eamonn Holmes hosts the quiz featuring contestants representing groups and societies that have benefited from National Lottery grants. Plus the midweek draw.

9.00 BBC News
With Michael Buerk. Regional News Weather with Sarah Wilmshurst Followed by National Lottery Update

9.30 The Boy David – the Return
David was discovered in a Peruvian hospital with the centre of his face eaten away by a cancerous condition called noma. He was then adopted by an eminent plastic surgeon who began the process of rebuilding David's face. Over the last 18 years Desmond Wilcox has followed his progress with five award-winning films, and this sixth instalment finds him as a 25 year old art student embarking on a dangerous journey back to Peru to thank the people for the gift of life. **See Choice.**

10.30 The X Files
The cult series starring David Duchovny and Gillian Anderson. *Drive*. Following Mulder's abduction at gunpoint by a man suspected of killing his wife, Scully tries to determine whether the kidnapper is suffering from an infectious disease. These investigations lead her to uncover a deadly government experiment. **See Choice.**

11.15 Children of Crime
An episode from the series tracing the history of juvenile crime. *The Mary Bell Case*. An investigation into the murder of two young boys by an 11-year-old girl in 1968. Followed by **Weatherview**

12.10 The Haunting of Helen Walker
A governess discovers that the children in her charge are haunted by the ghosts of their nanny and valet.

BBC2

8.00
Financial wizard Alvin Hall dispenses gilt-edged advice on effective money management to people facing currency crises in Your Money or Your Life

6.00 TOTP2
The pop-music show raids the archives for performances from Madness, Elton John, the Sweet, Sonny and Cher, M People and Dire Straits. With Steve Wright

6.45 Star Trek: Deep Space Nine
Waltz. A seriously injured Sisko is stranded on an unknown plant, accompanied by a prisoner awaiting trial whose behaviour is becoming increasingly irrational.

7.30 Best of Enemies
The second of two programmes in which former cabinet minister Kenneth Baker studies cartoons to shed light on Britain's relationships with two continental neighbours. Baker looks at the traditionally stereotypical images of Germans in British cartoons and travels to Germany to discover their cartoonists' impressions of us.

8.00 Your Money or Your Life
Financial expert Alvin Hall returns for a new six-part series as he helps more people to overcome their cash crises. Tonight he meets three London-based Malaysian sisters whose extravagant lifestyle has outgrown their income, leaving them all in considerable debt. **See Choice.**

8.30 Looking good
The fashion-and-health show comes back for a seven-part series. Lowri Turner receives hair and skin-care advice from John John Gustafson and Anthony Yacomine, two viewers undergo a week's detox diet, plus a guide to the January sales and a look at new year fashions.

9.00 Home Front in the Garden
Diarmuid Gavin heads to Wolverhampton to create a modern, bright garden for a couple with an 18-month-old daughter. Among the features included in his design are a peaceful rooftop retreat, a child's play pit brimming with plastic balls, a giant television wall, and a very modern garden gnome. Introduced by Tessa Shaw.

9.30 The Creatives
The comedy set in the offices of an Edinburgh advertising agency returns for a second, six-part series. *She Was the One*. After 17 years, Ben realises that he married the wrong woman and decides to look up an old flame. Robbie faces the prospect of sacking an employee.

10.00 The Fast Show
Another chance to see the third series of the sketch show. With Paul Whitehouse, Caroline Aherne, Simon Day, Charlie Higson, John Thomson, Arabella Weir and Mark Williams.

10.30 Newsnight
With Jeremy Paxman. At 11.00 News headlines

11.20 World Darts
Highlights of the last four second-round matches at the World Professional championship.

12.00 Despatch Box
Parliamentary analysis, with Michael Dobbs.

12.30 BBC Learning Zone

ITV CARLTON

7.00
Pollard (Chris Chittell) receives an unwelcome warning from Graham (Kevin Pallister) as harsh words are exchanged in tonight's **Emmerdale**

6.00 Regional news magazine
PM Followed by **Regional Weather; Travel Talk**

6.30 ITV Evening News
Weather John Hammond

7.00 Emmerdale
Turner convinces Diane to back Bernice, Betty has a secret assignation, and Graham and Pollard clash.

7.30 Coronation Street
Les confronts Jez and finds out the truth about Leanne, while Gwen and Jim have a heart-to-heart talk.

8.00 Goodnight Mister Tom
Another chance to see this Bafta Award-winning wartime drama, starring John Thaw. At the outbreak of the Second World War, nine-year-old London evacuee Willie Beech is billeted on a surly widower, Tom Oakley. Tom soon realises that his charge has suffered physical and mental damage at the hands of his mother. **See Choice**

10.00 The Krays – Inside the Firm
Concluding this two-part documentary on the Krays and their alleged role in the murder of Frank Mitchell. Krays' sidekick Freddie Foreman was acquitted of the murder of Mitchell for lack of evidence. But tonight he reveals he was the killer and describes how he carried out the murder while at the same time putting friendly senior Scotland Yard officers off the scent.

11.00 ITV Nightly News
Weather John Hammond

11.20 Regional News: Weather

11.30 The Big Match: Worthington Cup Highlights
Highlights of tonight's semi-final, first-leg match between Bolton Wanderers and Tranmere Rovers and the delayed quarter-final clash between Leicester City and Fulham.

12.35 Back of Beyond
Romantic thriller. After he survives a motorbike accident in which his sister dies, Tom McGregor neglects the garage and diner they ran together. Years later, trouble finds him when three criminals stop off to repair their vehicle.

2.10 A Chorus of Disapproval
Comedy, based on Alan Ayckbourn's play, starring Anthony Hopkins and Jeremy Irons. A lonely widower lands a part in an amateur production of The Beggar's Opera and finds himself susceptible to the charms of other cast members.

4.00 Wish You Were Here?

4.30 Judge Judy More legal disputes.

4.50 ITV Nightscreen Text-based information

5.30 ITV Morning News Ends 6.00am

CHANNEL 4

10.30
Man of many faces: a new series combining comedy, drama and documentary reveals the phenomenon known as **That Peter Kay Thing**

6.00 Shipwrecked
A nine-part documentary series in which 16 people aged 24 and under are sent to a small uninhabited South Pacific Island called Moturakau to fend for themselves for ten weeks. Today, the group arrive on the island and build their shelter.

6.30 Hollyoaks
Lucy has to face the inquest into Rob's death, Nikki returns from hospital, and Cindy is confronted about Holly's money

7.00 Channel 4 News
With Jon Snow, Krishnan Guru-Murthy. **Weather**

7.55 Voices on the Line
Following a funeral in Ghana, a 40-day process that culminates in a celebratory farewell to the deceased.

8.00 Brookside
Katie, Mike and Rachel decide to move into Sinbad's house. Shelley convinces Jackie to talk to Lindsey.

8.30 The Real Holiday show
This week, Emma Kennedy meets twin brothers who are going for a week's break in Benidorm, and an amateur photographer visits Tenerife with three glamour models.

9.00 Cracker
Police drama starring Robbie Coltrane, with Robert Carlyle. *To Be a Somebody* (Part 1). Following the murder of an Asian shopkeeper, the police start searching for a racist skinhead, but Fitz is convinced they are on the wrong track.

10.00 Smack the Pony
The contemporary, irreverent comedy sketch series with Fiona Allen, Doon MacKichan and Sally Phillips.

10.30 That Peter Kay Thing
A six-part spoof fly-on-the wall documentary series in which Peter Kay plays 15 different characters. *In the Club*. Brian Potter – the owner of a social club – organises a committee meeting to discuss a cabaret night.

11.05 Best Friends
Tonight's programme is about the friendship between two 30-year-old women – one of whom is HIV positive.

11.35 Stand Up Perrier
A showcase of some of the best acts from the 1999 Edinburgh Fringe Festival, including Al Murray's Pub Landlord.

12.40 The End of America
An exploration of Miami, the southernmost US city and a place with extremes of affluence and poverty.

2.05 Rasputin, the Mad Monk
Horror. Rasputin, an unscrupulous Russian monk, hypnotises two officials of the tsar's court in order to gain access to the tsar and his power. Widescreen.

3.40 A Rage in Harlem
Crime thriller. A gangleader's mistress arrives in fifties' Harlem hoping to sell some stolen gold.

5.30 Countdown Game show. Ends 5.55am

CHANNEL 5

6.00 5 News

6.30 Family Affairs
Julie-Ann is suspicious of Pete's motives for helping Cat and Dave

7.00 The Movie Chart Show
Gail Porter presents more film news and reviews

7.30 Nick's Quest
Anaconda. Nick Baker finds the world's largest snake in the Venezuelan region of Llanos.

8.00 Floyd around the Med
Tonight Keith Floyd travels to Corfu to cook a culinary delight inspired by his surroundings and washed down with the local wine.

8.30 Hollywood's Airport
First in a six-part documentary series about the work of the immigration workers at Los Angeles international airport. Today, a famous dog is booked a first-class plane ticket.

9.00 The Shooter
Thriller starring Dolph Lundgren. Arriving in his native Prague to arrest a professional hit woman, a US Marshal begins to suspect that the assassin is innocent and that he is an unwitting player in a deadly conspiracy

11.00 Family confidential
Docu-soap series revealing peoples' extraordinary lives. Tonight, a couple who are both porn actors and like to bring their work home.

11.50 The Comedy Store
Stand-up comedy from the Comedy Store in London, with Scott Capurro, Paul Zenon, Andy Parsons and Marcus Brigstocke.

12.20 AM Live and Dangerous Ends 5am
NHL Ice Hockey Phoenix Coyotes v Pittsburgh Penguins

4.00 NHL Ice Hockey
Highlights of Phoenix Coyotes v New York

WEDNESDAY 12 January

TELEVISION

Whereas television fiction is seen to be based on acting, it is 'factual' programmes like the news and documentaries that are thought to be most real. News is discussed in the next chapter (on pages 52–4) but what about documentaries?

Documentaries

A documentary is a programme that aims to present the truth about a subject. The 'truth' can be coded or represented in many different ways.

ACTIVITY

Compare two different documentaries on television (such as on politics, science, natural history) by answering the following questions.

1 Where does the information come from (for example, a presenter, narrator's voice-over, interviews with experts, statistics, the public, and so on)?
2 Are any sound effects or music used?
3 What kind of narrative is there – is there a puzzle being solved, a story told, a debate between differing views developed, or a straight description of details?

The fact that there is no one way of making a documentary suggests that there is no one way of being able to capture the truth about the world. Film and television always involve choices that mean **interpretations** of what is happening.

One style of documentary that some people claim is the closest to being 'real' has been called the **'fly on the wall'** (or cinema vérité) film. Documentary series have been made on the police, schools, the armed forces, prisons and even family life using this approach.

Source 2.18

1 Why is 'fly on the wall' filming so called?
2 Do you think people act naturally once they get used to cameras?
3 Very little voice-over commentary is provided to explain things to the viewer. Does this mean the viewer is more able to make up his or her own mind about what is being shown?

The 'fly on the wall' or to coin a phrase 'télé verité' school of documentaries grew up in the sixties and seventies, helped greatly by technical improvements. Crews who had once dragged round huge cameras and enough lighting equipment to illuminate Wembley Stadium were given cameras which fitted snugly on one man's shoulder, and which had lenses and film stock capable of picking up images in almost anything short of total darkness ... Directors dislike the tag 'fly on the wall' which they say makes them appear secretive; they prefer the phrase 'piece of the furniture', which implies something so familiar that it is invisible but largely ignored ...

The cameraman must provide long, uninterrupted tracking shots and capture fast-moving scenes without any chance of a retake ... It was the apparently straight forward nature of the technique which helped persuade Thames Valley to left Graef and Stewart in. Mr Harry Ross, the acting Deputy Chief Constable, says that by showing police work as it really is, they hoped to dispel the most persistent accusation against them: that they are a closed, secretive organisation which hangs together and protects its own ...

Most directors claim that men subjects, whether policemen, sailors, public school boys or prisoners, tend to become increasingly oblivious as filming goes on, though they never entirely forget that the camera is there. Roger Mills, whose unit made 'Sailor', 'Strangeways' and 'Hospital' among others of the genre, says that it depends on what the person is doing. 'If a fireman is up a ladder taking a suicide down, he obviously isn't speaking to the camera. But if he's chatting in a small room, he is bound to be more conscious.' ...

It all boils down, as with most forms of journalism, to the director's own honesty and, without being snide, it is fair to say that most BBC directors share an unswerving and enviable belief in their own integrity ... This integrity gets its toughest test in the editing, and a clue to this is the 'shooting ratio' – the amount of film consumed by the cameras compared to the amount which winds up on the screen. In a conventional documentary this is around 9 or 10 to 1, in 'télé-verité' it is nearer 20 to 1, and 'Police' would have come in at 30 or 40 to 1, if the series had not been lengthened. The key to the finished programme is of course, which inches the director chooses from the yards available ...

With hindsight, several of the Thames Valley officers now think they would have preferred a commentary. Those we spoke to did not actually criticise the editing, but they felt that crucial links had been omitted – usually for legal reasons or because even two crews could not cover all aspects of a complicated case.

This tallies with the experience of Mr Barry Irving who is the director of studies at the Police Foundation, an independent research body. He spent nine months observing police interrogations for the Royal Commission on Criminal Procedure and reckoned that 'after a few weeks' the officers became used to his presence and were unaffected by it.

However, he says that 'Police' has to be regarded chiefly as entertainment, since the prime time television excludes serious exploration of the context and setting ...

Source 2.18 (*The Observer*, 24 January 1982, on the making of *Police*)

Reality television

This is a label that has been increasingly applied to all those programmes that seemingly allow ordinary people access to appear as themselves. 'Real-life', or sometimes reconstructed scenes are used, often recorded on the new generation of lightweight but high-grade video camcorders. In practice, the label covers a wide variety of programmes that might feature ordinary people as:

Source 2.19 (*Broadcast*, 26 June 1998)

1 subjects in a professionally produced 'fly on the wall' documentary (as described above);
2 subjects of entertainment in spontaneous home videos, such as *You've Been Framed*;
3 subjects in dramatised reconstructions, such as *999*;
4 amateur director in a personalized documentary of an event or way of life, such as *Video Diaries*.

Question for group discussion

Which of these forms of 'reality television' is most likely to contain a genuine representation of ordinary people's lives?

We might add a fifth category to the above, which is the **docusoap**. This is where a television production team has selected real people whose lives can be shown in a short serial that resembles a

LAKESIDERS

Producer: Hart Ryan Productions

Broadcaster: BBC 1

Start: 20.30, 13 July

Length: 8 x 30 minutes

Commissioned by: Peter Salmon

Executive producers: David Hart,

Stephen Lambert

Series producer: Guy Davies

BY ESTHER ELEY

If BBC documentaries executive producer Stephen Lambert was looking for a follow-up to BBC 1's Airport, he couldn't have done better than Lakesiders.
The series, produced by Hart Ryan Productions, puts the microscope on the Lakeside Shopping Centre in Essex – Europe's busiest mall, heaving with 24 million shoppers each year.
'We were looking for something with a great throughput of people and good potential for drama,' says Lambert of his latest show. And if people see his approach as veering perilously close to BBC soap EastEnders, then he's only too pleased.
'We see the Lakeside as a huge Queen Vic that draws our characters together,' he says, adding: 'We're out to really play up the connection – we even got Simon Mayo, the guy who wrote the music for EastEnders, to write ours.'
Lakeside is a Queen Vic of monster proportions, and researcher Jenny Byrom had

her work cut out when she began canvassing potential participants for the series. 'We started a year ago, going into every shop and speaking to the staff,' explains Byrom. 'There's 330 shops in all so it was an almighty task.'
For series producer Guy Davies, getting to film inside the stores was his first hurdle, with many worried about how the series would affect their image. 'The big stores particularly needed reassurances. It's amazing how sensitive they are,' Davies says.
The next step was finding the right cast of characters to make the docu-soap grip viewers week after week.
'We had to be clear early on about exactly what mix of characters we were going for,' Davies days. 'The scattergun approach, where you hope it will come out all right in the editing room, only spells disaster.'
While filming, it quickly became apparent that watching people shop or following shop assistants with cameras would make for dull viewing.

The solution was for researcher Jenny Byrom to find staff with eventful lives outside work, such as the gutsy blonde perfume girl who tries to make it as a singer and has her wedding plans called off. Following an undercover store detective was the biggest scoop of the series, according to Isaacs, who says that filming without disputing the detective's work took some ingenuity. 'I'd use a wide-angle lens or a zoom and make myself invisible – standing behind potted plants and all that,' he recalls.
Of course, you can't film people without their permission, so when Richard first moved in on someone, I'd be filming everything from his perspective. Then, as he was confronting the person, I would make myself known and capture it on film.'
'We intended to produce something that was a cross between Cutting Edge, Airport and EastEnders and that's exactly what we've got.'
Source 2.19, Broadcast, 26 June 1998

soap opera. Docusoaps like *The Cruise* and *Airport* have proved to be extremely popular with audiences (and there is the bonus that they are much cheaper to make than conventional soap operas because there are no actors and scriptwriters to pay!)

Source 2.19

1 What seem to be the main ingredients for a successful docusoap?
2 To what extent can a series such as *Lakesiders* claim to be documentary?

An alternative to filming people in their natural environment is to select ('audition') your cast of subjects and control the conditions within which they are filmed. This is one step further away from traditional documentary and towards scripted entertainment.

Source 2.20

1 Is the format of *The Living Soap* likely to be effective as a way of representing ordinary student life?
2 What alternative forms of television could be used to give an insight into student life?

Some television writers and producers prefer to represent real-life events and people within a fictional dramatic form with actors, music and so on. This might produce a stronger emotional response from the audience, in contrast to the more subdued approach of a documentary (see Figure 2.3 on page 34).

There is thus no one superior way of representing the real world, and the degree of realism achieved is very much dependent on the response of audiences, who will have very different judgements of whether or not the truth of a situation has been captured. Much also depends on the motivations of the media producers – whether the intention is primarily to entertain or to inform.

Source 2.20 (*The Guardian*, 9 October 1993)

Real life neighbours

Just a normal student house. Except for fire doors, smoke alarms and TV cameras.
ROBERT LEEDHAM meets the students turned TV stars in BBC2's The Living Soap

The house is owned by the BBC. There's an editing suite in the basement. The students were handpicked; the girls are sexy the guys are funny. But this claims to be a stab at 'reality television' – part Video Diaries, part The Young Ones, with a dash of Sylvania Waters and a dab of Beverley Hills 90210 thrown in for good measure.

In return for letting themselves be filmed au natural, the six students – Simon, Emma, Karen, Matthew, Dan and Vidya, who prefers to be called Spider – have been given, rent-free, an enormous, rambling house on the outskirts of Manchester. It's far superior to most student accommodation, but then there are going to be up to four camera crews inside at any one time, and one wouldn't want them bumping into each other.

Producer Spencer Campbell comes to the show via The Word, The Krypton Factor and Coronation Street, and admits that the programme, like any other fly-on-the-wall documentary, will only be able to show an edited version of real life. In fact, he intends to manipulate events to create mini-plots and cliffhangers for the end of each episode. The Living Soap will be a true hybrid. 'We won't alter the pattern of events,' he says, 'but we might delay things …'

The six students have absolutely no editorial control over their screen personas. And with up to 60 hours of filmed footage being whittled down each week to make one half hour programme, that's quite a gamble. 'They could stitch us up,' agrees Karen, 'but I don't think they will, to be honest. We're free to walk out at any time; they wouldn't want that. I think they like us enough not to do it.'

Figure 2.3 (Granada annual report, 1995)

DRAMA
Documentaries

BREAKTHROUGH
AT REYKJAVIK

HOSTAGES

104 Mins

Between March 1985 and January 1987, Terry Anderson, Tom Sutherland, Brian Keenan, John McCarthy, Frank Reed and Terry Waite were kidnapped in the Lebanon by the fundamentalist Muslim group Hezbollah. The last of these hostages was not freed until December 1991. For years they were kept in the most squalid conditions, chained, constantly beaten and threatened with death. **Hostages** is a powerful new drama-documentary that dramatises the story of how the men survived and how the four women in their lives campaigned tirelessly to gain the release of their loved ones. Stars Kathy Bates, Colin Firth, Ciaran Hinds, Natasha Richardson, Jay O Sanders, Josef Sommer and Harry Dean Stanton.

A Granada Television/HBO Showcase Production.

HOSTAGES

THATCHER –
THE FINAL DAYS

THATCHER –
THE FINAL DAYS

52 Mins

Sylvia Syms plays the role of Britain's former Premier Margaret Thatcher in a re-creation of the events leading up to her defeat as party leader and resignation as Prime Minister. All the key parliamentary figures involved in the leadership battle are portrayed. Written by a team of specialist writers following months of careful research.

Granada

Figure 3.1b

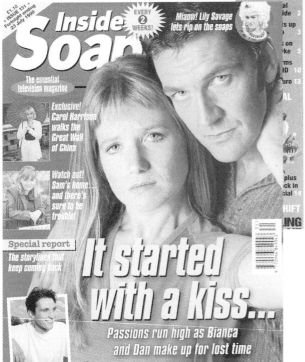

Figure 3.1a

BROADCAST
THE WEEKLY NEWSPAPER OF THE TELEVISION AND RADIO INDUSTRY
2 JULY 1999   £2.30

THIS WEEK

Dyke looks to popular drama to revive BBC 1

BY STEVE CLARKE

Greg Dyke, the new BBC director general, will put popular TV drama under the spotlight as part of a strategy aimed at strengthening the appeal of BBC 1.

More money is likely to be earmarked for mainstream drama series in a policy that could echo Dyke's approach to bankrolling popular small screen fiction when he ran LWT 10 years ago.

A source said: 'One of the ways Greg helped turn round LWT and ITV in the late 1980s and early 1990s was to invest heavily in returnable drama series for the 21.00 slot.

'Greg may attempt to do something similar when he arrives at the BBC.'

Dyke is understood to be an admirer of much BBC drama and rules out any reduction in the range of material.

He has told colleagues that serials such as last autumn's critically acclaimed *Vanity Fair*, shown on BBC 1, are central to the corporation's remit. What concerns him, however, is the lack of hits and flair in staple ongoing series.

How drama is commissioned and produced will form part of a review Dyke is planning for the entire BBC production process. He wants to discover how well the split between

BBC Broadcast and Production is working and is known to be sceptical about some of its alleged benefits (see box).

Dyke also intends to appoint a sports supremo, working across all areas of the corporation, to help reclaim rights to high-profile sports events.

In an interview with *Broadcast*, the director general designate denied he had 'a master plan' for the BBC. He said: 'I do not go in with a master plan. I have no plans to bring in loads of people and get rid of people.

'My position is straightforward. I will go round and talk to a lot of people. I will ask them what they think.'

Dyke storms the Beeb, p14

BROADCAST/PRODUCTION RETHINK

The news that Greg Dyke plans to review the Broadcast/Production split will be   in-house or indie ideas. But, unlike indies, BBC producers had nowhere else to go if

Figure 3.1c

music week
For Everyone in the Business of Music   9 APRIL 1994   £2.80

Playlists to rule R1

THIS WEEK

Radio One controller Matthew Bannister is tightening his grip on the station's music policy by dramatically increasing the daytime output controlled by the playlist.

In a radical overhaul of the station's music selection process, 67 of every 100 records aired during the 10 daytime shows will be dictated by the playlist committee – an increase of more than 26%.

Bannister is promising more new music and more far three more records in the new playlist structure, but pluggers fear the changes will create a less flexible Radio One.

music Radio One plays will be increased by his decision to replace the 'C' playlist with an 'N' list of 10 tracks, primarily by new artists. Each record will be guaranteed nine plays a week and a four-week run on the playlist.

Overall the changes will increase new music output from 24% to 31%, while oldies will be slashed from 36% to 30%, says Bannister.

'We have modelled ways of rotating records and have arrived at a system we think will work,' he says.

'In the past the rotation levels were not always achieved and the rotation of the 'C' list was far too low.'

When you switch on television to watch a particular programme, you will have certain expectations: that the programme will start and finish at specific times, that it might contain particular pleasures for you as a viewer, that if you do not enjoy it you will switch channels or turn off and so on. In other words, watching television is an activity about which there are shared ideas, meanings and practices – it is an **institution**. We see it as a normal part of everyday life, like reading a newspaper, listening to the radio, shopping or going to school.

Without an audience, television would cease to have any point. Likewise, without television production, there would be nothing for audiences to watch. What brings media producers and audiences together, and how is the relationship between them shaped? This is the study of media as an institution.

MEDIA AS AN INDUSTRY

Media products can be compared to any other product sold to the public – washing machines, cars, breakfast cereals and so on. The aim is to sell as many units as possible and achieve the greatest profit for the owners.

Cinema

The Hollywood studios have always been run as businesses. One of the ways of making a profit has been to use particular actors and actresses. If they are packaged as **stars**, then their films are likely to be popular. Stars in the cinema are performers who become more than mere actors in the eyes of the audience. They are thought to possess something extraordinary, beyond everyday normality. Star quality is usually built up by other media (especially the press and magazines), by presenting them as special people. This is often in response to box office success.

Although television performers may be referred to as stars – such as David Jason or Cilla Black – they do not share the same sense of extraordinariness or glamour as film stars. Those appearing on television tend to have a more familiar and cosy relationship with audiences.

ACTIVITY

Look at some film or pop music fan magazines (such as *Total Film*, *Smash Hits*, and so on), select an example of a current star performer and describe how he or she is represented. What kind of image is being constructed? Compare this to the representation of a television personality in the *Radio* or *TV Times*, or the entertainment pages of the popular press. What kinds of pictures are used? How are they described? What aspects of their private life are discussed?

' *From a business point of view, there are many advantages in the star system. The star has features that can be advertised and marketed – a face, a body, a pair of legs, a voice, a certain kind of personality, real or synthetic – and can be typed as the wicked villain, the sweet young girl, the neurotic woman. The system provides a formula that is easy to understand and has made the production of movies seem more like just another business. The use of this formula may serve also to protect executives from talent and having to pay too much attention to the quality of a story or of acting. Here is a standardized product that they can understand, that can be advertised and sold, and that not only they, but also banks and exhibitors, regard as insurance for large profits.*

Source 3.1 (H. Powdermaker, *Hollywood the Dream Factory*, Little, Brown, 1950)

HOLLYWOOD REPORTER 'STAR POWER' LIST 1999

1	Tom Hanks	11	Nicholas Cage
2	Mel Gibson	12	Arnold Schwarzenegger
3	Tom Cruise	13	Jack Nicholson
4	Harrison Ford	14	Will Smith
5	Jim Carrey	15	Bruce Willis
6	Leonardo DiCaprio	16	Meg Ryan
7	John Travolta	17	Clint Eastwood
8	Julia Roberts	18	Jodie Foster
9	Robin Williams	19	Sean Connery
10	Brad Pitt	20	Sandra Bullock

Sources 3.1 and 3.2

1 Why do you think there are only four actresses in the top 20?
2 Choose three stars from the list and write a short account explaining why you think each star is so popular with audiences. It will be helpful to start with a list of their most successful films – this might reveal the kinds of roles and types of film in which they are likely to appear.

Source 3.2
Hollywood Reporter's star power list for 1999 is based on a survey of those working in the film industry (worldwide). They are asked to rank stars on their ability to ensure a film's profitability.

The Press

Sources 3.3a and b

After examining a range of tabloid and broadsheet newspaper front pages, identify what methods newspapers use to boost circulation apart from their choice of news stories.

Source 3.3a (*The Mirror*, 2 November 1999)

Source 3.3b (*Daily Mail*, 2 November 1999)

Advertising and newspapers

All newspapers depend to some extent on advertising income. Between 20 and 40 per cent of the content of national daily newspapers consists of advertising. This proportion may be as high as 66 per cent of the Sunday supplement magazines. Increasingly, local newspapers are becoming dependent on advertising, as can be seen by the number that are delivered free of charge to houses. These are called freesheets.

The effect on choice

Source 3.4 *Newspapers, class and advertising*

1 Why do the broadsheet daily and Sunday newspapers not need to sell so many copies?
2 How do the tabloid daily and Sunday newspapers gain most of their income?
3 Which readers seem to have the greatest choice of newspapers?

Figure 3.2 The changing face of *The Sun*

> The original *Sun* newspaper dates from the last century. The current *Sun* started as the *Daily Herald* in 1912 as a paper for the Labour movement. After reaching over 2 million circulation in the 1930s, its sales declined to 1.3 million when it was relaunched as *The Sun* in 1964. It continued to decline (to 1 million) until Rupert Murdoch took over in 1969. He introduced the version similar to today, which rose to a circulation of 4 million within 10 years.

(T. Douglas, *The Complete Guide to Advertising*, Guild.)

National newspaper circulation		Social class of readership	Percentage revenue from sales	Percentage revenue from advertising
Dailies				
The Sun	3,672,284	mainly working and lower middle	73	27
The Mirror	2,353,905			
Daily Record	640,776			
Daily Star	616,759			
The Express	1,063,891			
Daily Mail	2,398,073			
The Daily Telegraph	1,044,606	mainly upper middle	42	58
Financial Times	411,409			
The Guardian	397,177			
The Independent	222,776			
The Scotsman	77,059			
The Times	742,511			
Sundays				
News of the World	4,170,112	mainly working and lower middle	69	31
Sunday Mail	765,128			
Sunday Mirror	2,002,028			
Sunday People	1,577,849			
Sport First	91,678			
Sunday Express	977,146			
Mail on Sunday	2,330,135			
Independent on Sunday	246,162	mainly upper middle	34	66
The Observer	416,091			
Scotland on Sunday	116,705			
Sunday Business	58,553			
Sunday Telegraph	826,288			
The Sunday Times	1,361,094			

Source 3.4 ABC, September 1999

Television

Gaining large audiences is also important for television. In the case of commercial television (all television apart from the BBC), these are needed to attract advertisers who buy airtime from the television companies (see Table 3.4). The highest rates are charged for advertising during those programmes with the largest audiences.

The BBC does not have advertising. Instead, its income is mainly derived from the licence fee charged to every household with a television set. However, in order to justify the licence fee, it is important for the BBC to maintain a good share of the audience – about 30–40 per cent.

The sizes of audiences for particular programmes are described as **ratings** (see page 111). These figures, which are published weekly, show which are the most popular programmes in order. In America, they are so important that a series may be cancelled after two or three weeks if its ratings are poor.

The way to obtain high ratings is to produce programmes that have broad popular appeal, and then ensure they are broadcast at a time that is likely to achieve the biggest audiences. This is the art of **scheduling**.

General cost of advertising

Television advertising is a commodity, therefore the capital cost is dependent on the number of advertisers wishing to purchase airtime. Prices are related to demand as supply is fixed at an average of seven minutes commercial airtime per hour. November and the first two weeks of December are invariably the most expensive times to mount an advertising campaign as advertisers are keen to promote their products to attract Christmas shoppers.

Airtime is sold using rate cards, which are structured to deliver a share of television advertising revenue proportionate to the size of the television transmission area.

Variations in price occur dependent on the time of transmission, viewing figures, number of advertisers in the same product field, time of year and so on.

To ensure an advertising campaign works, the campaign has to be seen by an audience. Audience delivery is measured in ratings. Television ratings (known as TVRs) are defined as the percentage of a particular audience that have seen a commercial break – that is 10 adult TVRs = 10 per cent of all adults in the Granada area who have tuned in.

Target audiences are homes, housewives, adults, men, women, children. These groups can then be broken into further subgroups, so an advertiser can successfully target businesspeople, men aged 16–34 and so on.

At the negotiation stage it is agreed by the advertiser/advertising agency and TV contractor how many TVRs the campaign needs to achieve. A campaign price is then agreed.

A rough guide to the cost of advertising on Granada Television			

When advertising agencies buy campaigns for clients, they usually need 200–300 ratings (TVRs) – this would equate to roughly 20–25 separate spots. These spots would be spread across the day and week, hopefully seen by as many different people as possible.

To give you a very rough idea of actual cost, details of three spots are given below.

Station: Granada ITV
Month: February 1998
Target audience: Adults
Length: 30 seconds

Programme	Time	Rating	Cost
This Morning	11.00	4	£754
Granada Tonight	18:15	14	£3,525
McCallum	21.20	17	£4,706

Table 3.1 (*Granada media sales 1998*)

Source 3.5

Using a television listings guide, see if you can find examples to illustrate the key principles of scheduling.

ACTIVITIES

1 Examine the BBC and ITV schedules for the week in a TV listings magazine. Select what you think is a strong BBC and a strong ITV evening's schedule. Suggest reasons for your choice.

2 Imagine you are the controller of television scheduling for an evening between 6.00 and 11.00pm for either ITV or the BBC. Create a schedule of programmes that you think would gain the largest audience. Try to include a varied mixture – that is, avoid bunching together programmes of a similar kind, such as soap operas and comedies.

Source 3.6

What appeal do you think these programmes have for viewers in other countries?

Programme sales

Selling programmes to other countries is an increasing source of revenue for television companies. In fact, many television productions are now international (for example British-American co-productions). This means that greater financial backing can be achieved and the end product can be sold to more than one country.

Programmes that are successful in Britain do not necessarily sell well abroad. For example, *Coronation Street* has only three regular subscribing countries – Canada, Ireland and New Zealand.

TV SCHEDULING: TRICKS OF THE TRADE

HAMMOCKING
The practice of sticking a potentially weak, sagging programme between two stout, dependable rating pullers in the hope that the viewers will be too lazy to switch channels. However, with the remote and the growth of channels it's much easier to get out of hammocks these days. So schedulers don't do it any more. They have too much respect for the power of the viewer, they say.

PAIRING
For example, C4's recent 'Coked Up' pairing put two documentaries on cocaine back-to-back. It is, of course, impossible to say whether the shows would have had worse ratings if screened separately but they definitely attracted more coverage and enabled the channel to provide more effective trailing. Pairing should not be confused with attempts to make something look more than the sum of its parts. Schedulers just wouldn't do that.

THEMING
Two's company, three's a theme. Like pairing, only more so. Again, not to be confused with attempts to stick chaff in with the wheat. Heaven forbid.

STRIP AND STRAND
Having the same programmes or genre at the same time every day, much loved by listing mag designers. Its attraction is that you know exactly where you are (usually lying on the sofa at three in the afternoon watching Cagney and Lacey).

'STUNT' SCHEDULING
A pejorative term used by public service broadcasters to describe commercial television's ad hoc attempts to boost ratings. Usually involves stranding Who Wants To Be A Millionaire? across the week or having daily helpings of Emmerdale or Corrie. Not to be confused with week-long daily helpings of EastEnders.

ZONING
Zones are really just regular theme nights. The key to their success is that viewers know where they are. Friday night is BBC 2 and C4's comedy night, Saturday evening is BBC 2's History Zone.

Source 3.5 (*Broadcast*, 21 January 2000)

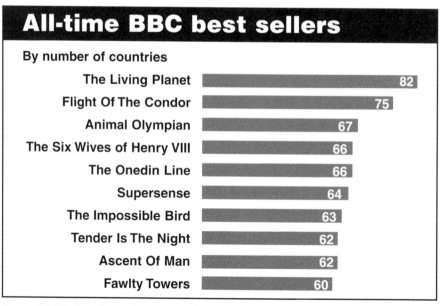

All-time BBC best sellers

By number of countries

The Living Planet	82
Flight Of The Condor	75
Animal Olympian	67
The Six Wives of Henry VIII	66
The Onedin Line	66
Supersense	64
The Impossible Bird	63
Tender Is The Night	62
Ascent Of Man	62
Fawlty Towers	60

Source 3.6 (*The Guardian*, 23 February 1998)

Source 3.7

1 Which television genres (or types) are most successful in achieving high television ratings?

2 Are these genres scheduled at particular times (of the day and week)?

Multimarketing

Apart from making money via sales of media products (cinema tickets, CDs and so on) and associated advertising, there is another important, and growing, source of profit. This is the sale of goods that are somehow tied in with the original media product. The process of recycling or extending a media product into other forms is referred to as **multimarketing**.

One well-established method of multimarketing is via licensed merchandising. Disney has been doing this for over 50 years with its films, but in recent years it has become a huge moneyspinner. The original *Star Wars* (1977) is often credited with being the first film to really merchandise on a large scale. It is estimated that the first three *Star Wars* films generated over $2 billion in merchandising. The 1999 *Star Wars* release – *Star Wars: The Phantom Menace* – was predicted to make over $4 billion in merchandising, via the computer game, Pepsi, toy figures, Lego models and so on. Many films are planned with the aim of simultaneously launching merchandising, especially toys – for example, *Toy Story* and *Tarzan*.

Another method of multimarketing is to develop related media products. With respect to films, this often involves releasing a music soundtrack that not only makes money in the form of sales of CD singles or albums but also helps to promote the film, as Celine Dion's *My Heart Goes On* from *Titanic* did.

Top 50 weekly series: winter season 1999

Title	Average audience (millions)	Weeks on air	Change % from winter 98	Share (%)	Network licensee & indie producer	Usual day	time	Prog type•	Status*
1 Coronation Street	16.19	17	−1.3	63	ITV (Granada)	M/W/F/Sun	1930	D SO	c
2 A Touch of Frost	15.84	4	–	59	ITV (Yorkshire)	Sun	2000	D S	r
3 Heartbeat	15.75	8	1.6	57	ITV (Yorkshire)	Sun	2030	D S	r
4 Who Wants/Millionaire?	14.88	3	–	54	ITV (Celador)	Mon-Sun	2000	L G	N
5 EastEnders	13.56	17	−3.7	54	BBC 1	M/T/Thu	1930	D SO	c
6 Forgotten	11.70	3	–	46	ITV (LWT)	Mon	2100	D SR	N
7 Emmerdale	11.58	17	−1.0	51	ITV (Yorkshire)	T/W/Thu	1900	D SO	c
8 Casualty	11.54	10	−16.7	44	BBC 1	Sat	2005	D S	r
9 Airline	11.35	7	−1.1	44	ITV (LWT)	Fri	2000	F DO	r
10 Police, Camera, Action!	11.21	3	−0.6	44	ITV (Carlton/Optomen)	Thu	2030	F DO	2/r
11 Neighbours From Hell	10.79	5	14.8	42	ITV (Central)	Fri	2030	F DO	r
12 London's Burning	10.76	8	−10.3	43	ITV (LWT)	Sun	2100	D S	r
13 Where The Heart Is	10.45	3	6.0	42	ITV (Anglia)	Sun	2000	D S	r
14 Peak Practice	10.19	13	2.7	41	ITV (Central)	Tue	2100	D SR	r
14 Ground Force	10.19	12	–	42	BBC 1 (Bazal)	Fri/Sun	2000	F DO	r/2
16 Stars in Their Eyes	10.11	8	6.9	45	ITV (Granada)	Sat	2020	L V	r
17 Kavanagh QC	9.98	4	1.7	43	ITV (Central)	Mon	2100	D S	r
18 Antiques Roadshow	9.80	11	31.0	40	BBC 1	Sun	1845	F DO	r
19 Better Homes	9.72	10	–	38	ITV (Granada)	Mon	2030	F DO	N
20 The Bill	9.59	16	8.0	39	ITV (Thames)	Tue/Thu	2000	D S	C
21 Tilly Trotter	9.55	4	–	38	ITV (Festival)	Fri	2100	D SR	N
22 This is Your Life	9.51	9	−2.1	40	BBC 1 (Thames)	Mon	1900	L R	r
23 The Vice	9.47	6	–	38	ITV (Carlton)	Mon	2100	D S	N
24 Holby City	9.32	9	–	35	BBC 1	Tue	2000	D S	N
25 Blind Date	9.14	16	10.0	42	ITV (LWT)	Sat	1900	L G	r
26 Sunburn	8.81	6	–	36	BBC 1	Sat	2055	D S	N
27 National Lottery Draw	8.62	7	17.0	36	BBC 1	Sat	1950	L R	c
28 Tarrant on TV	8.56	12	−6.7	41	ITV (LWT)	Sun/Fri	2200	L O	r/2
29 We've Got Your Number	8.46	9	–	37	BBC 1	Sat	1950	L R	N
30 The Knock	8.43	6	–	35	ITV (LWT/Bronson Knight)	Thu	2100	D S	r
31 Parking Wars	8.38	6	–	37	ITV (LWT)	Fri	2000	F DO	N
32 Play Your Cards Right	8.19	12	−2.8	39	ITV (LWT/Fremantle)	Fri	1900	L G	r
33 Changing Rooms	8.16	14	−21.8	31	BBC 1 (Bazal)	Wed	2000	F DO	r/2
34 Last Train	8.09	4	–	34	ITV (Granada)	Thu	2100	D SR	N
34 Cop Shop	8.09	7	–	33	ITV (Tiger Aspect)	Mon	2030	F DO	N
36 Vets in Practice	8.02	5	−10.3	32	BBC 1	Tue/Thu	2000	F DO	r
37 Wish You Were Here...?	7.98	16	−0.4	39	ITV (Thames)	Mon	1900	F DO	r
38 Animal Hospital	7.97	7	−16.3	33	BBC 1	Tue/Thu	2000	F DO	r
39 They Think It's All Over	7.87	3	–	38	BBC 1 (TalkBack)	Thu	2205	L GC	r
40 Britain's Worst ...	7.83	6	–	33	ITV (Lion)	Fri	2100	F DO	N
41 Family Fortunes	7.72	6	0.7	30	ITV (Central)	Sat	2010	L G	r
42 Harbour Lights	7.69	9	–	31	BBC 1 (Valentine)	Thu	2000	D S	N
43 My Kind of Music	7.68	8	−2.3	34	ITV (LWT)	Sun	1830	L G	r
44 Last of the Summer Wine	7.64	7	–	34	BBC 1	Sun	1815	L SC	2
45 Scarlet Pimpernel	7.60	4	–	28	BBC 1	Sun	2000	D S	N
46 Last of the Summer Wine	7.46	3	−8.5	30	BBC 1	Sun	2000	L SC	r
47 The Generation Game	7.43	4	−0.8	36	BBC 1	Sat	1800	L G	r/2
48 Holiday/On A Shoestring	7.40	15	−6.8	32	BBC 1	Tue	1900	F DO	r
49 Playing the Field	7.32	7	−8.2	33	BBC 1 (Tiger Aspect)	Thu	2135	D SR	r
50 Only Fools and Horses	7.24	4	−1.2	33	BBC 1	Fri	2000	L SC	2
Averages	9.62	8	−1.5	40					

• D Drama, DO Documentary, informative, F Factual, G Gameshow, GC Comedy game, L Light ent, O TV clips, R 'Reality' entertainment, people shows, S Series, SC Sitcom, SO Soap, SR Serial, V Talent contest
* N New, r Returning, c Continuous, 2 Repeat

Source 3.7 (William Phillips, *Broadcast*, 18 June 1999)

ACTIVITY

Complete the table using your own examples of media products that have been developed via other media forms. Try to choose one original example for each media form.

Title	TV series	Film	Magazine/ comic	Computer video game	Music
X Files	Original	✓	✓	✓	✓

THE MEDIA AND BIG BUSINESS

Concentration of ownership

Fewer and fewer companies control the majority of media production. In Britain, in 1998, the top four companies in each area of media production accounted for:

- 95 per cent daily newspaper circulation;
- 72 per cent music album sales;
- 65 per cent audiences for independent television (non-BBC);
- 51 per cent magazine circulation.

Many of these companies have interests in more than one area of the media, as well as owning other types of companies. Such large organizations are called **conglomerates**. The publisher of this book, Pearson Education, is part of the Pearson conglomerate, which has business interests that include the *Financial Times*, Thames Television, Channel 5 and Penguin Books.

Source 3.8 (News Corporation Annual Report, 1999)

The News Corporation Limited W o r l d w i d e

Television

United States
FOX Broadcasting Company (a)
Fox Television Stations (a)
22 local TV stations
Twentieth Television (a)
FOX News Channel (a)
FX (a)
Fox Sports Networks (a)
    (Interests in 21 regional sports networks)
Regional Programming Partners (b) (40%)
    (Regional cable sports channels, Radio City Music Hall, New York Knicks, New York Rangers, MSG Network and Madison Square Garden arena)
National Sports Partners (b) (50%)
National Advertising Partners (b) (50%)
The Health Network (b) (50%)
FOX Sports World Espanol (b) (50%)
The Golf Channel (b) (33%)
Home Team Sports (b) (34%)
CTV Sportsnet (b) (20%)
Outdoor Life (b) (34%)
Speedvision Networks (b) (34%)
Fox Family Worldwide (b) (49.5%)
    Fox Family Channels
    Fox Kids Network
    Fox Kids Europe
    Fox Kids Latin America
    Fox Kids International Networks
    Saban Entertainment
fXM: Movies from Fox (a)
TV Guide Networks (44%)
TV Guide Interactive (44%)
TV Games (44%)
Echostar Communications Corporation (13%)

United Kingdom
British Sky Broadcasting (40%)

Germany
VOX (49.9%)
TM3 (66%)

Italy
Stream (35%)

Latin America
Canal Fox (a)
Fox Sports Latin America (b) (50%)

Australia and New Zealand
FOXTEL (25%)
Sky Network Television (25%)

Asia and China
STAR TV
Phoenix Satellite Television Company Ltd. (45%)
    Phoenix Chinese Channel
    Phoenix Movies Channel
Tianjin Golden Mainland Development Company Ltd. (60%)
ESPN STAR Sports (50%)
Channel [V] Music Networks (60%)
VIVA Cinema (50%)

India
Asia Today Ltd. (50%)
    ZEE TV
Programme Asia Trading Co. Pvt. Ltd. (50%)
    ZEE Cinema
    ZEE News
Siticable Network Pvt. Ltd. (50%)

Japan
News Broadcasting Japan (80%)
Sky Entertainment Corporation (50%)
Sky Movies Corporation (50%)
Sky PerfecTV! (11%)

Filmed Entertainment

United States
Fox Filmed Entertainment (a)
    Twentieth Century Fox
    Fox 2000 Pictures
    Fox Searchlight Pictures
    Fox Animation Studios
    Fox Music
    Twentieth Century Fox Home Entertainment
    Twentieth Century Fox Licensing and Merchandising
Fox Interactive
Twentieth Century Fox Television
Fox Television Studios

Australia
Fox Studios Australia (b) (50%)

Mexico
Fox Studios Baja (a)

Magazines and Inserts

United States and Canada
TV Guide Magazine Group (44%)
    TV Guide
    TV Guide Ultimate Cable
        TV Guide Ultimate Satellite
    The Cable Guide
    See
The Weekly Standard
News America Marketing
    In-Store
    FSI (SmartSource™ Magazine)
News Canada Marketing
    planet U (30%)
    SoftCard Systems, Inc. (22%)

Book Publishing

United States, Canada, United Kingdom & Europe and Australasia
HarperCollins Publishers

Newspapers

United States
New York Post

United Kingdom
The Times
The Sunday Times
The Sun
News of the World
The Times Educational Supplement
The Times Higher Education Supplement
The Times Literary Supplement
Nursery World

Australia
(more than 100 national, metropolitan, suburban, regional and Sunday titles)

New Zealand
Independent Newspapers Limited (49.7%)
    (nine daily, two national Sunday and more than 40 suburban and community newspapers and 14 national magazines in New Zealand; and three regional newspapers in Australia)
Pacific Islands Monthly

Fiji
The Fiji Times
Nai Lalakai
Shanti Dut

Papua New Guinea
Post-Courier (63%)

Controlling the market

The manufacture of pop music

As long as the pop music industry has existed, there have been attempts by the music companies to carefully guide the teenage and pre-teen music audience into buying their latest 'product'. This has led to accusations that pop stars have been 'manufactured'. In more extreme cases, music groups have been artificially brought together and packaged to fit a certain image thought likely to succeed. An example from the 1960s is that of the Monkees, a manufactured American version of the Beatles. The group was provided with songs and a television series in order to market the band effectively.

How much control?

It is possible to exaggerate the influence that big business interests have on the media. The ability to control the market and determine the choice of product available to audiences is limited by several factors – not least, the unpredictability of demand. A remarkable example of a film succeeding against the odds is *The Blair Witch Project*, which cost $35,000 to make and yet took $50 million during its first week of showing in America in 1999.

Fresh from Mr Spice!

This Thursday, a new comedy-drama begins on children's BBC. It's called *Miami 7*, and it follows the adventures of a 'loud, wild, fresh, ballsy, sexy' pop group called S Club 7 ... After the 13-part series and the records there will be another 13-part series. And after that, a feature film will be coming soon to a cinema near you. Meanwhile, S Club 7 fans will be enrolled in an international youth organisation linked by the group's website.

S Club 7 is the brainchild of Simon Fuller. And Simon Fuller was the manager of the Spice Girls. It was he who marketed them with a vigour that the music business had never seen before. It was he who had them endorsing cameras, selling their own range of toys and advertising crisps and Pepsi and Channel 5. Without him, there might never have been a Spice Girls deodorant.

His collaborators on the project are Initial TV –

makers of *Get Your Act Together* and the televising of the Brit Awards – not to mention an army of writers, producers and web-page designers. The S Club 7 Internet site will soon be up and running, and it in turn will be the linchpin of the most novel part of the operation. The 'Club' in S Club 7's name is there for a reason. Fuller and co are hoping to raise the concept of the fan club to a new level. Members won't just receive newsletters and badges; they'll join an interactive society, conceived as an up-to-date rival of the Scout movement.

While all this was being prepared, Fuller has had yet another matter to attend to: forming the band. 'We didn't just want seven actors,' says Henry of the auditions. 'We wanted maybe two who had really good voices, two who could dance, one who was into fashion, one who was the big brother figure ...' Not since Take That has a manufactured group had its

division of labour calculated so logically.

With ages ranging between 16 and 22, S Club 7 has someone for everyone ... Now meet S Club 7. There's Jon, 16, an *EastEnders* alumnus and 'a total romantic'; there's Hannah, 17, and as bubbly as a bottle of Vimto – 'life's always a bit of a party when she's around'; there's Bradley, 17, the black clubber, and 'most definitely a laydeez man'; there's Jo, 19, who has already had a minor hit single in Germany, and is 'loud, full-on and a bit mad'; there's Rachel, 20, a model who 'could shop all the time'; there's Tina, 22, a professional dancer and 'confessed shopaholic'; and there's Paul, 22, a heavy rocker with 'a grown-up head on his shoulders'. Allow me to be the first person to ask you: who's your favourite S Clubber? I won't be the last.

Source 3.9 *Independent on Sunday*, 4 April 1999

Studio executives

Studio executives are intelligent, brutally overworked men and women who share one thing in common with baseball managers: they wake up every morning of the world with the knowledge that sooner or later they're going to get fired …

They are responsible for what gets up there on the silver screen. Compounding their problem of no job security in the decision-making process is the single most important fact, perhaps, of the entire movie industry:

NOBODY KNOWS ANYTHING.

Not one person in the entire motion picture field knows for a certainty what's going to work. Every time out it's a guess – and, if you're lucky, an educated one …

Raiders is the number-four film in history as this is being written. I don't remember any movie that had such power going in. It was more or less the brainchild of George Lucas and was directed by Steven Spielberg, the two unquestioned wunderkinder [wonder boys] of show business (Star Wars, Jaws, etc.). Probably you all knew that. But did you know that Raiders of the Lost Ark was offered to every single studio in town – and they all turned it down?

All except Paramount.

Why did Paramount say yes? Because nobody knows anything. And why did all the other studios say no? Because nobody knows anything. And why did Universal, the mightiest studio of all, pass on Star Wars, a decision that just may cost them, when all the spin-offs and toy money and book money and video game money are totalled, over a billion dollars? Because nobody, nobody – not now, not ever – knows the least goddam thing about what is or isn't going to work at the box office …

And they had passed on E.T.

Columbia had had it, developed it for a million dollars, took a survey, and discovered the audience for the movie would be too limited to make it profitable. So they let it go. (Universal picked it up and may make back the billion they didn't earn by dropping Star Wars.) …

Source 3.10 (William Goldman, *Adventures in the Screen Trade*, Macdonald, 1984)

INDEPENDENT MEDIA PRODUCTION

There are always new media producers vying for a place in the market. When these producers exist outside of large mainstream media business organizations, then they can be said to be **independent**.

In comparison with the mainstream media corporations, independent media production is characterised by:

- smaller scale of organization;
- more risk-taking and experimentation with new ideas;
- specialist knowledge and expertise;
- closer involvement with the audience.

However, there is no clear way of defining 'independent production' as the label is used in a variety of contexts – for example, independent television (not relying on a licence fee), *The Independent* newspaper (not having a political leaning). Furthermore, it is often the case that 'independents' are partly dependent on major companies to operate effectively – to reproduce and distribute the product (magazines, music tapes, etc.) to high street retailers, for example.

The case of pop music

Ever since the beginning of the rock'n'roll era in the mid 1950s, the music industry has regularly failed to predict audience demand. New music styles have tended to be championed by independent labels, from Sun Records, rockabilly and Elvis Presley to rap, trance and other dance music. Using cheap and easily accessible new technology, such as samplers, mixers and DAT cassette recorders, it is possible to produce for just a few hundred pounds a single or album that can then be distributed to independent record shops, clubs, radio stations, and so on.

Source 3.11

Compare the current network and independent charts (for example in *New Musical Express*).

1 What impact are the independent labels having on the network charts?
2 How do the charts differ in terms of music styles?

Independent magazines

Small-scale independent publishing has always been popular, going back to the last century in the case of newspapers. Left-wing radical newspapers and the likes of *The Northern Star* were able to achieve a readership of 500,000 by the 1850s. Exceeding that in terms of readers is the case of *Viz*, which at one stage in the early 1990s had a circulation of over one million, having begun as a comic sold in a few pubs and shops in Newcastle a few years earlier.

More typical of independent magazines are **fanzines** – largely produced by and for fans of specialist areas of popular culture neglected by mainstream publications. Music and football fanzines have been particularly successful in the last 20 years and, like all independent publishers, have been able to take advantage of developments in technology, especially desktop publishing (see page 63 for a case study).

ACTIVITY

Try to obtain a fanzine and write a profile of the magazine based on your research into its origins, distribution and typical readership.

SIZE ISN'T EVERYTHING

Contrary to what the music corporations would have us believe, the history of rock'n'roll has been largely written by small independent labels. It's unlikely, for instance, that Elvis Presley would have come to the attention of RCA had he not first recorded for Sun Records, while early rock'n'roll and R&B was dependent on labels such as Chess and Specialty.

In that pioneer era, the scale of American operations was largely determined by the huge distances involved in distribution: each city would have its own local labels – Sun in Memphis, King in Cincinnati, Chess and Vee-Jay in Chicago, Speciality and Aladdin in Los Angeles, Excello in Nashville, Duke in Houston – which would develop local hits; the most

successful records would then be picked up and promoted nationally, sometimes through distribution affiliations with larger companies. Accordingly, a record could take months to build up enough momentum to chart, compared with the instant, blanket coverage of today.

In the Sixties and Seventies, companies such as Island and Elektra developed strong label profiles through coherent A&R policies, while Frank Zappa, with his Bizarre, Straight and DiscReet imprints, pioneered the trend for artists to form their own labels, still going strong today through the likes of Prince's Paisley Park and – on a smaller scale – Howie B's Pussyfoot.

As rock had become progressively more fractionalised, independent labels

have continued to trace the cutting-edge of developments in each genre: soul (Stax, Atlantic, Hi, Curtom); jazz (Blue Note, Impulse!, CTI, ECM) new wave (Rough Sub Pop), rap (Tommy Boy, Def Jam, Sugarhill); reggae (Trojan), post-rock (Kranky, Drag City), world music (Globestyle, World Circuit, Realworld, Rykodisc, Luaka Bop) and, of course, an immense swathe of labels tracking the dance scene (XL, JBO, Warp, Skint, Mo'Wax, Perfecto, Ninja Tune etc).

But by far the most encouraging indication of the enduring health of the independent sector is the traditional folk outlet Topic Records, currently celebrating no less than 60 years of serving the nation's acoustic needs. Happy birthday!

Source 3.11 Andy Gill *The Independent* 28 May 1999

Figure 3.3 Football fanzines

General laws applying to the media

Media products are controlled by laws, including the following.

The Official Secrets Act

Originally, this was designed to stop secrets going to possible enemies of the State, and the Act was very wide-ranging. Although in 1989 it was made more specific, it still covers a broad area of information that is meant to ensure that journalists reveal little or nothing about the security services, defence and the conduct of international relations.

Libel

The libel law exists to protect anyone against unfair or damaging public statements. It is most often used against newspapers, as in the case of Elton John who was paid £1 million compensation by *The Sun* in 1988 for making false allegations.

Contempt of court

This prevents the media reporting anything that might mean someone will not receive a fair trial.

National emergency

This mainly applies during war. For example, during World War II the Prime Minister, Winston Churchill, banned the *Daily Worker* (a Communist newspaper) for fear it would harm national unity. During the 1982 Falklands War, some government censorship was exercised: only officially approved journalists were allowed to travel with the armed forces, and all media reports were vetted by the Ministry of Defence before being made public. The Gulf War in 1991 was subject to similar restrictions, although there were satellite pictures and reports from inside the 'enemy' state of Iraq.

The media were expected to side with the Allied Forces (the Gulf Task Force) in their quest to liberate Kuwait.

Obscene Publications Act

This is a very controversial law that has been used mainly in relation to sexually explicit material ('that which is likely to deprave or corrupt') appearing in magazines, films and videos. In 1990, it was extended to all the media, including television and pop music.

Media regulations

Cinema

Cinema films and, more recently, videos are subject to the approval of the British Board of Film Classification before being made available to the public. The Board categorizes films as U, PG, 12, 15 or 18 (see Figure 3.4 for video classification). The main guideline is whether or not a film or video would 'offend against good taste or decency' and, in the case of a video, whether it is 'suitable for viewing in the home' or not.

ACTIVITY

Compare a 15-certified video with one that has a PG certificate. Try to identify the reasons for the different classifications for the two videos.

Broadcasting

To broadcast in Britain requires a licence. Two organizations have had the right to provide television and radio services: the BBC (since 1926) and the Independent Broadcasting Authority (IBA), (since 1955). Between them they controlled all national and local television and radio in Britain until the 1980s.

The BBC helped establish the principle that television in Britain should provide more than just entertainment –

Stuart Millar and Janine Gibson on a new series featuring three homosexuals which has provoked moral outrage over a plotline involving a boy of 15, but has won the praise of equality campaigners

Two of a kind . . . Aidan Gillen and Craig Kelly in Queer as Folk: 'After the first episode there's not much sex in it'

Channel 4 glad to pioneer the first gay drama on British TV

Figure 3.5 (*The Guardian*, **24 February 1999**)

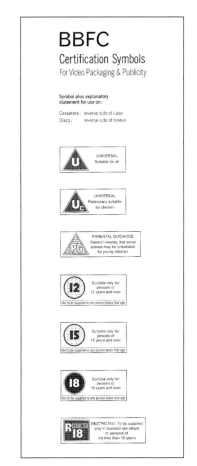

BBFC

Certification Symbols
For Video Packaging & Publicity

Symbol plus explanatory statement for use on:

Cassettes: reverse side of case
Discs: reverse side of sleeve

U — UNIVERSAL Suitable for all

Uc — UNIVERSAL Particularly suitable for children

PG — PARENTAL GUIDANCE General viewing, but some scenes may be unsuitable for young children

12 — Suitable only for persons of 12 years and over. Not to be supplied to any person below that age

15 — Suitable only for persons of 15 years and over. Not to be supplied to any person below that age

18 — Suitable only for persons of 18 years and over. Not to be supplied to any person below that age

R 18 — RESTRICTED. To be supplied only in licensed sex shops to persons of not less than 18 years

Figure 3.4

it should operate as a **public service**, meaning that information and education should also be important features of what is broadcast. This public service concept is not among the aims of many other countries' television stations. The BBC's charter has been extended to 2006, with the aim of its becoming an international media company. Profit from commercial activities abroad – such as from satellite news channels – may be an alternative source of income to the current licence fee. The fee has to be paid by all households with a television set, thus ensuring that the BBC does not have to show advertisements. The licence fee will continue, at least until 2006.

The public service principle was extended in 1982, when Channel 4 was introduced with a special remit to provide both new types of programmes and programmes for a wider range of audiences that might previously have been neglected, such as gays and lesbians (Figure 3.6).

Independent Television Commission

The IBA was replaced by the Independent Television Commission (ITC) in 1991, following the Broadcasting Act 1990. Its main function is to issue licences and regulate all television services in Britain other than the BBC. Its first main duty was to oversee the awarding of ITV franchises in 1991, which were given to those companies who made the highest cash bid while ensuring a high quality of service to viewers. Although exercising a 'lighter touch' than the IBA over the content of programmes broadcast on the network, the ITC is still able to threaten

companies who are seen as falling below acceptable levels of quality (see Figure 3.6). For example, in 1998 the ITC imposed a £2 million fine on Central TV for broadcasting a documentary, *The Connection*, which contained faked scenes of drug smuggling. Figure 3.7 illustrates how ITV (Channel 3) output meets the minimum requirements of the Broadcasting Act 1990.

Meanwhile, the BBC's right to broadcast on the basis of funding by the licence fee, rather than advertising like ITV, depends on its ability to offer a specially valuable service to viewers and listeners. It has set out its purpose as 'extending choice for viewers and

listeners by guaranteeing access for everyone in the country to programme services that are of unusually high quality'. In particular, it promises to offer:

- a wide range of news, current affairs and information programming;
- fresh and innovative entertainment and a showcase for both traditional and modern British culture;
- specialist and general programmes that help to educate their audience;
- programmes and services that communicate between the UK and the rest of the world.

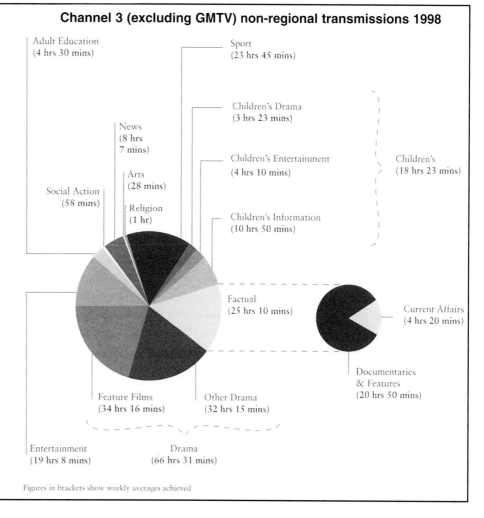

Quality, range and diversity of programmes

The Broadcasting Act 1990 requires a sufficient amount of programmes of high quality in regional Channel 3 services. It also mandated five categories of programmes for which the ITC had to set minimum amounts when the Channel 3 licences were advertised in 1991. These were regional programmes (including Gaelic programmes in Scotland), national and international news, current affairs, children's programmes and religious programmes. The minimum amounts in the other four categories were as follows:

- **national and international news** 3 programmes each weekday of 20 minutes (lunch time), 15 minutes (early evening) and 30 minutes in peak time;
- **current affairs** 1 hour 30 minutes weekly average;
- **children's** 10 hours weekly average;
- **religion** 2 hours weekly average.

Channel 3 (excluding GMTV) non-regional transmissions 1998

Adult Education (4 hrs 30 mins)

Sport (23 hrs 45 mins)

Children's Drama (3 hrs 23 mins)

News (8 hrs 7 mins)

Children's Entertainment (4 hrs 10 mins)

Children's (18 hrs 23 mins)

Arts (28 mins)

Social Action (58 mins)

Religion (1 hr)

Children's Information (10 hrs 50 mins)

Factual (25 hrs 10 mins)

Current Affairs (4 hrs 20 mins)

Documentaries & Features (20 hrs 50 mins)

Feature Films (34 hrs 16 mins)

Other Drama (32 hrs 15 mins)

Entertainment (19 hrs 8 mins)

Drama (66 hrs 31 mins)

Figures in brackets show weekly averages achieved

Figure 3.6 (*ITC Annual Report*, 1998)

Radio Authority

The Broadcasting Act 1990 also established the Radio Authority, which has three main tasks:

1 to widen listening choice;
2 to protect the listener from biased, offensive and inaccurate material;
3 to help radio stations increase their audience size and profits by allowing them more freedom in choosing what to broadcast and how much to advertise.

The first aim, greater listening choice, has been pursued by granting three national radio licences – to Classic FM, Virgin and Talk Radio – and by extending the number of local radio stations, particularly specialized services.

Table 3.2 (*BBC Annual Review, 1998–9*)

Other Regulatory Bodies

Press Complaints Commission (PCC)

This replaced the Press Council in 1991 and was designed to improve the standard of newspaper journalism without resorting to new laws. Its members include a number of newspaper editors, and its main role is to enforce a code of practice agreed by all the national and regional newspaper editors covering areas such as accuracy, harassment (such as persistent questioning) and invasion of personal privacy (such as using long-lens cameras). Any newspaper found guilty by the PCC of breaking the code following a complaint from the public is required to print the PCC's findings 'in full and with due prominence' – not hidden away in small print.

The PCC has made several criticisms of tabloid newspapers for their publication of intimate details of members of the Royal family, such as private telephone conversations of both Prince Charles and Diana, the late Princess of Wales. As a result, new laws have been proposed that would forbid them from publishing such stories. However, the key issue is whether or not the story is something the public have a right to know – 'in the public interest' – rather than simply being what the public are interested in.

Broadcasting Standards Commission (BSC)

This body has two main functions. First, to give guidance to all broadcasters on issues of fairness and privacy and standards of decency and taste. Second, to review complaints made against broadcasters by those who have either been offended or dealt with unfairly. Table 3.2 shows the number of complaints made by the public about individual programmes and advertisements during 1998.

Advertising Standards Authority (ASA)

This was set up in 1962 to ensure that advertisements appearing in Britain (other than on television and radio) are 'legal, decent, honest and truthful'. The Authority issues a Code of Advertising Practice and if it thinks an advertisement is unacceptable because it is misleading or in poor taste, the advertiser will be told to change or remove it. Only rarely are its instructions ignored, an example being Benetton, criticized in 1992 for including a man dying of AIDS as part of its campaign to sell clothes.

Programmes and ads attracting large numbers of complaints:	Numbers of complaints
Queer as Folk (part 1)	110
Jude (film)	35
The South Bank Show (31.1.99)	32
Men Behaving Badly (25.12.98)	19
Vice – The Sex Trade (16.11.98)	16
Ad for Levis	25
Ad for Lucozade	18
Ad for *Heat* magazine	16

Note: In addition to individual programmes, one series, *The Lakes*, attracted 150 complaints.

Sources 3.12a and b

Why might the ASA have criticized
these two advertisements?

Source 3.13

Why do you think this advert caused offence, particularly among black people?

Adverts causing most controversy are
those that are seen as offending against
good taste (see Figure 3.8 on page 51).
During the 1990s, Benetton launched
several advertising campaigns that
provoked considerable numbers of
complaints, resulting in several of their
adverts being withdrawn. Initially,
Benetton's adverts tackled the issue of
race relations in their United Colors
campaign, the intention being to
promote racial harmony. However their
choices of images did not always cause
the public to arrive at this interpretation.

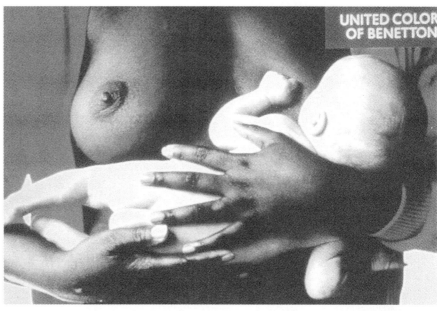

Source 3.13

Source 3.12a

Source 3.12b

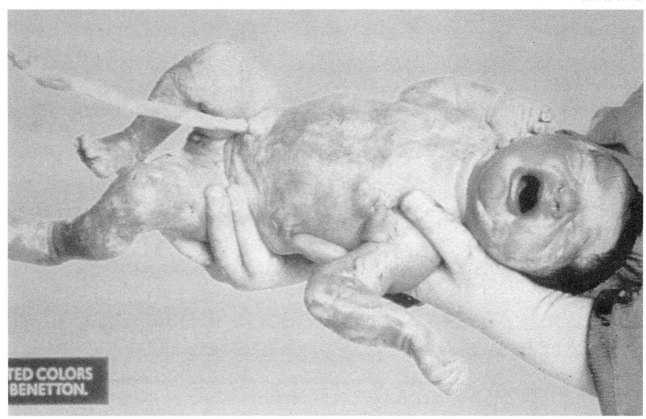

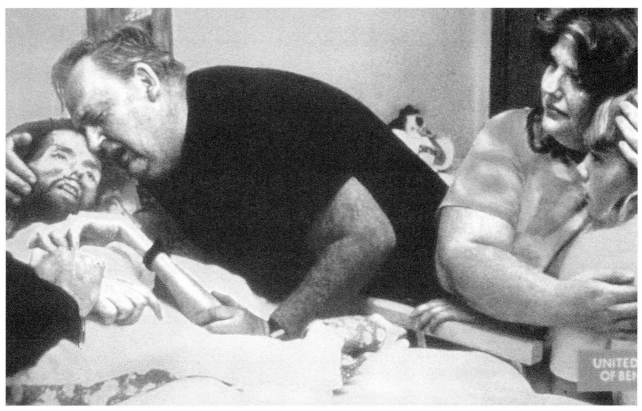

While the Advertising Standards Authority did not uphold complaints against the advert of the baby being breast-fed, they did ask Benetton to withdraw two subsequent adverts (source 3.14) following a large number of complaints when they were published in 1991. The second advert shows a man dying of AIDS (permission to use the photo having been granted to Benetton by the man's parents). The stated aim of Benetton's campaign was to 'overcome cultural barriers and human indifference' – in particular to stimulate debate about the world's problems.

Sources 3.14 a and b

With reference to the ASA decency code (shown in Figure 3.8) and Benetton's advertising aims, consider the arguments for and against banning the Benetton adverts.

The products most stringently controlled by advertising codes are cigarettes and alcohol (Figure 3.9).

Decency

No advertisement should contain any matter that is likely to cause grave or widespread offence. Whether offence is likely to be caused and, if so, of what gravity, will be assessed in each case in the light of the standards of decency and propriety that are generally accepted at present in the United Kingdom.

The fact that a product may be found offensive by some people is not, in itself, a sufficient basis under the Code for objecting to an advertisement for it. Advertisers are urged, however, to avoid unnecessary offence when they advertise any product which may reasonably be expected to be found objectionable by a significant number of those who are likely to see their advertisement.

Figure 3.7 (Advertising Standards Authority)

ACTIVITY

Collect some current adverts for alcoholic drinks and examine whether or not they might be guilty of breaking the ASA code as outlined in Figure 3.8

ALCOHOLIC DRINKS

46.1 For the purposes of the Codes, alcoholic drinks are those that exceed 1.2% alcohol by volume.

46.2 The drinks industry and the advertising business accept a responsibility for ensuring that advertisements contain nothing that is likely to lead people to adopt styles of drinking that are unwise. The consumption of alcohol may be portrayed as sociable and thirst-quenching. Advertisements may be humorous, but must still conform with the intention of the rules.

46.3 Advertisements should be socially responsible and should not encourage excessive drinking. Advertisements should not suggest that regular solitary drinking is advisable. Care should be taken not to exploit the young, the immature or those who are mentally or socially vulnerable.

46.4 Advertisements should not be directed at people under 18 through the selection of media, style of presentation, content or context in which they appear. No medium should be used to advertise alcoholic drinks if more than 25% of its audience is under 18 years of age.

46.5 People shown drinking should not be, nor should they look, under 25. Younger models may be shown in advertisements, for example in the context of family celebrations, but it should be obvious that they are not drinking.

46.6 Advertisements should not feature real or fictitious characters who are likely to appeal particularly to people under 18 in a way that would encourage them to drink.

46.7 Advertisements should not suggest that any alcoholic drink can enhance mental, physical or sexual capabilities, popularity, attractiveness, masculinity, femininity or sporting achievements.

46.8 Advertisements may give factual information about the alcoholic strength of a drink or its relatively high alcohol content but this should not be the dominant theme of any advertisement. Alcoholic drinks should not be presented as preferable because of their high alcohol content or intoxicating effect.

46.9 Advertisements should not portray drinking alcohol as the main reason for the success of any personal relationship or social event. A brand preference may be promoted as a mark of the drinker's good taste and discernment.

46.10 Drinking alcohol should not be portrayed as a challenge, nor should it be suggested that people who drink are brave, tough or daring for doing so.

Figure 3.8 (CAP)

The existence of such a range of external controls from the government and regulatory bodies significantly restricts the freedom of media professionals and organizations. To avoid unwanted interference or punishments, most people working in the media exercise self-regulation or operate their own in-house codes of practice.

MEDIA PROFESSIONALS

In any large organization, there is a division of labour, with special tasks being performed by those with the requisite skills and training. This means that the **owners** (usually the shareholders) are often not the **controllers** (those who decide what is made) or the **media professionals** (those who are employed to make television programmes, write newspapers and so on).

ACTIVITY

From any one of the main media, try to identify:

1 the different roles of those involved in producing a television programme, magazine, record or other media product (the key contributors are often mentioned in credit lists at the front of a magazine or at the end of a film or television programme, for example);
2 the different stages through which a product goes as it is assembled (a flow chart may be helpful here).

News production

Every individual joining an organization soon learns what is expected of them in terms of good practice and standards. This can be seen with the example of news production.

Sources

News does not simply flow into newsrooms. Much of it can be predicted and planned for in advance. Furthermore, some organizations can be relied on to supply a constant stream of stories, such as the police and courts.

Source 3.15

From a television or radio news bulletin or a national daily newspaper, try to identify as many of the sources of news as possible from the checklist below.

Sources mentioned routinely

1 Parliament
2 Councils
3 Police (and the army in Northern Ireland)
4 Other emergency services
5 Courts (including inquests and tribunals)
6 Royalty
7 'Diary' events (such as annual events like Ascot or conferences known about in advance)
8 Airports
9 Other news media

Organizations issuing statements and holding press conferences

10 Government departments
11 Local authority departments
12 Companies
13 Trade unions
14 Non-commercial organizations (pressure groups, charities and so on)
15 Political parties
16 Army, Navy, Air Force

Individuals making statements, seeking publicity and so on

17 Prominent people (such as politicians and film stars)
18 Members of the public

Source 3.15 (B. Whitaker, *News United*, Minority Press Group, 1981)

Processing and selection

Each day, those who produce the news have to decide which news should be covered, and how it should be presented. These decisions are often referred to as **gatekeeping**. There are several people who act as gatekeepers in processing the news on television, radio or in the press, from journalists up to senior editors.

1 From an evening's television or radio news, try to decide when each story has been selected during the day. One clue could be gained from recording and viewing news broadcasts throughout the day.

2 From a 12-hour cycle of news (from breakfast time to mid-evening), compile a chart showing how the running order of stories has changed.

News values

Deciding what to include in the news and which stories should be given most attention depends on their **newsworthiness**.

Some of the most important news values are:

- **drama/unexpectedness** – sudden, spectacular events;
- **personalities** – presenting news in relation to key individuals – the eye witness, the human survivor, famous celebrities, and so on;
- **relevance** – its importance for national and local interest – events happening far away have to be very dramatic to be covered;
- **immediacy** – things that have happened very recently;
- **continuity** – events that are part of a 'running story';
- **negativity** – bad news, disasters, threats and so on.

THE PRODUCTION CYCLE

News Sources	Selection	Gathering/Processing
Predicted news, Diary events, Parliament, Royalty, reports, trials and so on	The evening before	Camera/sound crews Reporters
News developments from predicted news and unexpected events	Editorial conference	Delivery and processing
	Rough running order	
	Planned running order	
		Editing, script writing and graphics
Late news	Rehearsal and final selection	
	News broadcast	

How they bring the news

1

9.00am • The producer of the day arrives in the newsroom. Already, between a third and a half of the programme has been 'blocked off' to make room for expected material. Today, for instance, Trevor McDonald will be sending a report on South Africa. There is also the TUC conference in Blackpool, an event which Channel Four News is bound to cover. There are several options for news material. Peter Sissons, the programme presenter, may interview trade union leaders, or reporters may send packaged (edited) material down the line to London.

2

10.30am • Both Channel Four News and Channel One (News at One, the 5.45 News and News at Ten) hold editorial conferences to decide which 'on-the-day' stories they will cover. Channel Four News sends an observer to the Channel One conference, to check what the Channel One programmes are doing. Channel Four News relies heavily on the 5.45 News for the 'hard news' for its summary. At the same time, Channel Four News will send its own crews on its own on-the-day stories.

3

2.30pm • Editorial conference, attended by the presenters, the home and foreign editors and senior editorial staff. There is a rough running order of items, but the top story is only provisional. Often a story's chances will depend on whether or not the programme can get an interview. When Dr Allan Boesak was arrested in Cape Town, Channel Four News needed to get a reaction from Desmond Tutu. This in turn depended on whether or not they could get a satellite link. In the event, link and interview went ahead.

4

4.30pm • A running order is circulated. The reporters are returning with their film. Now the process of assembly is underway, as people in charge of captions, slides, graphics, computer graphics, videotape editing and sound dubbing get to work on the 'packages', as the finished news items are called. There are almost 2000 different sound effects, from oars splashing to cars crashing. The most sought-after effect, curiously, is the sound of silence inside a house.

5

7.00pm • The programme goes on the air. The producer will not have seen how the whole thing looks until this moment. Only the top story is likely to have been rehearsed.

Right up to transmission, Channel Four News can deal comprehensively with late-breaking news (this is what really distinguishes it from *Newsnight*). The news of the football disaster at the Heysel Stadium broke five minutes before the producer of the day went down to the control room.

Source 3.16 Channel 4 News (*New Society*, 4 October 1985)

Broadsheet and tabloid newspapers have a differing emphasis in their news values, so it is unusual for a story to headline in both forms of newspaper – for example *The Times* and *The Sun*. Newspapers competing for the same type of reader often choose identical stories with which to lead the front page. In some cases this may even extend to using the same headlines (see Figure 3.9).

Visuals create another news value. Newspapers may run a story if they have an appropriate photograph to use. Television relies very heavily on visual images to go with its stories, whereas for radio this obviously does not matter.

Figure 3.9

How much freedom on music radio?

Media professionals rarely have the freedom to do as they please. Apart from having to work as part of a team, they have to consider the needs of their employers, the law and, not least, the audience. Which influence is most prominent varies according to the situation.

For example, DJs and producers on Radio 1 generally have much more freedom than their counterparts on independent local radio (ILR). This is particularly the case with Radio 1's evening and weekend programmes, where DJs such as John Peel can select their own personal choice of music. This is because the BBC as a public service broadcaster has a commitment to catering for as many musical tastes as possible, whereas ILR is under strong pressure to deliver audiences to advertisers and so is unwilling to risk its core audience switching off.

The limited choice for ILR producers and DJs is illustrated by the fact that most daytime music is selected by computer software! The computer is programmed to choose tracks from its memory, rotating them according to mood, tempo, energy and so on, from a **format** decided by the radio station. Formats are determined by the target audience of the service. A station seeking a broad audience of 20–40-year-olds would play a blend of current chart and past hits from the 1960s onwards. Many stations now use their AM and FM frequencies to offer alternative formats. Some of the most popular formats are described in Source 3.17.

Format	Music	Target audience age
Contemporary hit radio (CHR)	Current top 40 hits and very recent chart entries	15–34
Adult contemporary (AC)	Current and recent chart hits, excluding dance, metal, rap and other less 'easy' listening	25–44
Gold	'Classic' hits, especially from 1955–75	35–54
Easy listening (or light 'n' easy)	Nostalgic, melodic non-rock	45+

Source 3.17

ACTIVITY

Identify which music formats are employed by radio stations in your area.

Playlists

A radio playlist comprises those singles or album tracks that are guaranteed a minimum number of plays in any one week. ILR stations devise their playlists in accordance with their chosen format. Much more significant in terms of national airplay and chart success is Radio 1's playlist.

Radio 1's playlist comprises:

- A list = 20 tracks that receive between 25 and 32 plays per week;
- B list = 20–25 tracks that receive 10 to 20 plays per week;
- C list = 10–15 tracks that receive up to 7 plays per week.

Altogether, the playlist accounts for over half the output of shows up to 7pm on weekdays and between 4am and 10am at weekends. It is compiled by votes from senior producers in consultation with DJs (who can only make one personal selection of music within a three-hour show).

Source 3.18

1 What is the relationship between the Radio 1 and ILR playlists and the chart position of a single?
2 Does it seem to be necessary to be on the playlist to gain chart success?
3 Apart from radio airplay, how else can a single release become popular?

	new	**1**	**GENIE IN A BOTTLE** Christina Aguilera	RCA
new		**2**	**2 TIMES** Ann Lee	Systematic
1		**3**	**BLUE (DA BA DEE)** Eiffel 65	Eternal
new		**4**	**JESSE HOLD ON** B*Witched	Glow Worm/Epic
new		**5**	**GIVE IT TO YOU** Jordan Knight	Interscope/Polydor
3		**6**	**MAN! I FEEL LIKE A WOMAN!** Shania Twain	Mercury
2		**7**	**S CLUB PARTY** S Club 7	Polydor
6		**8**	**(YOU DRIVE ME) CRAZY** Britney Spears	Jive
5		**9**	**MAMBO NO 5 (A LITTLE BIT OF ...)** Lou Bega	RCA
10		**10**	**I TRY** Macy Gray	Epic
new		**11**	**I SAVED THE WORLD TODAY** Eurythmics	RCA
new		**12**	**FOREVER** The Charlatans	Universal
7		**13**	**SUN IS SHINING** Bob Marley vs Funkstar De Luxe	Club Tools
8		**14**	**WE'RE GOING TO IBIZA!** Vengaboys	Positiva
new		**15**	**EVERYTHING MY HEART DESIRES** Adam Rickitt	Polydor
9		**16**	**SUNSHINE** Gabrielle	Go Beat/Polydor
new		**17**	**JUST LIKE FRED ASTAIRE** James	Mercury
4		**18**	**GOIN' DOWN** Melanie C	Virgin
12		**19**	**THE LAUNCH** DJ Jean	AM:PM
16		**20**	**MICKEY** Lolly	Polydor
11		**21**	**THE AWAKENING** York	Manifesto
13		**22**	**BURNING DOWN THE HOUSE** Tom Jones & The Cardigans	Gut
17		**23**	**(MUCHO MAMBO) SWAY** Shaft	Wonderboy
15		**24**	**GET GET DOWN** Paul Johnson	Defected
new		**25**	**STAY WITH ME TILL DAWN** Lucid	ffrr
22		**26**	**ZORBA'S DANCE** LCD	Virgin
20		**27**	**BAILAMOS** Enrique Iglesias	Interscope/Polydor
new		**28**	**GIMME ALL YOUR LOVING' 2000** Martay feat. ZZ top	Riverhorse
23		**29**	**BETTER OFF ALONE** DJ Jurgen presents Alice Deejay	Positiva
27		**30**	**UNPRETTY** TLC	LeFace/Arista

Source 3.18 (Top 30 singles, *Music Week*, 16 October 1999)

Source 3.18 (Playlists, *Music Week* 16 October 1999)

RADIO ONE — BBC RADIO 1 97–99 FM

This	Last	Title Artist (Label)	Aud	LW	TW
1	11	**GIVE IT TO YOU** Jordan Knight (Interscope/Polydor)	20045	21	30
=2	4	**UNPRETTY** TLC (LaFace/Arista)	23488	31	29
=2	5	**SING IT BACK** Moloko (Echo)	22369	30	29
=4	3	**SUN IS SHINING** Bob Marley Vs Funkstar De Luxe (Club Tools/Edell)	22478	32	28
=4	2	**BLUE (DA BA DEE)** Eiffel 65 (Eternal)	22079	33	28
=6	6	**DRINKING IN L.A.** Bran Van 3000 (Capitol)	22134	28	27
=6	7	**OUT OF CONTROL** The Chemical Brothers (Virgin)	15178	26	27
8	14	**BUDDY X** Dreem Teem Vs Neneh Cherry (4 Liberty)	18844	18	26
9	14	**GENIE IN A BOTTLE** Christina Aguilera (RCA)	19557	18	24
=10	1	**GET GET DOWN** Paul Johnson (Defected)	20511	36	23
=10	21	**IN AND OUT OF MY LIFE** Onephatdeeva (Defected)	13121	14	23
12	13	**JUST LIKE FRED ASTAIRE** James (Mercury)	15508	19	20
13	new	**I TRY** Macy Gray (Epic)	14156	9	19
14	9	**S CLUB PARTY** S Club 7 (Polydor)	13760	24	18
=15	18	**STAY WITH ME TILL DAWN** Lucid (ffrr/Delirious)	12606	16	16
=15	new	**CARNATION** Liam Gallagher & Steve Cradock (Ignition)	10852	10	16
=17	28	**CLOSING TIME** Semisonic (MCA)	10665	12	14
=17	2	**2 TIMES** Ann Lee (Systematic/London)	8326	7	14
=19	25	**GA GA** Melanie C (Columbia)	10804	13	13
=19	18	**ON THE RUN** Big Time Charlie (Inferno)	9055	16	13
=19	new	**JUMP 'N' SHOUT** Basement Jaxx (XL Recordings)	6179	7	13
=22	new	**NEW DAY** Wyclef Jean/Bono (Columbia)	8861	6	12
=22	14	**THE LAUNCH** Dj Jean (AM:PM)	8578	18	12
=22	new	**LEARN TO FLY** Foo Fighters (RCA)	7680	8	12
=22	28	**BUG-A-BOO** Destiny's Child (Columbia)	7025	12	12
=22	new	**IN OUR LIFETIME** Texas (Mercury)	6848	10	12
=22	new	**SWASTIKA EYES** Primal Scream (Creation)	6362	6	12
=22	new	**JESSE HOLD ON** B*Witched (Epic)	4999	3	12
=29	21	**BURNING DOWN THE HOUSE** Tom Jones and The Cardigans (Gut)	9782	14	11
=29	28	**IF YOU HAD MY LOVE** Jennifer Lopez (Columbia)	9625	12	11
=29	new	**SEXXLAWS** Beck (Geffen)	8448	7	11
=29	21	**(YOU DRIVE ME) CRAZY** Britney Spears (Jive)	7972	14	11
=29	25	**COFFEE & TV** Blur (Food/Parlophone)	7914	13	11
=29	new	**SUNSHINE** Gabrielle (Go Beat)	7705	11	11
=29	17	**BETTER OFF ALONE** DJ Jurgen Pts Alice Deejay (Positiva)	7208	17	11
=29	new	**FOREVER** Charlatans (Universal)	6320	11	11
=29	new	**TURN IT AROUND** Alena (Wonderboy)	6139	6	11

© Music Control UK. Titles ranked by total number of plays on Radio One from 00.00 on Sun 3 Oct until 24.00 on Sat 9 Oct 1999

ILR

This	Last	Title Artist (Label)	Aud	LW	TW
1	1	**MAN! I FEEL LIKE A WOMAN** Shania Twain (Mercury)	49114	1890	2062
2	3	**UNPRETTY** TLC (LaFace/Artista)	40463	1637	1732
3	4	**BURNING DOWN THE HOUSE** Tom Jones And The Cardigans (Gut)	32002	1616	1648
4	6	**MAMBO NO 5 (A LITTLE BIT OF ...)** Lou Bega (RCA)	41825	1495	1644
5	2	**BLUE (DA BA DEE)** Eiffel 65 (Eternal)	35101	1694	1567
6	8	**GENIE IN A BOTTLE** Christina Aguilera (RCA)	33953	1315	1467
7	5	**(YOU DRIVE ME) CRAZY** Britney Spears (Jive)	26620	1515	1408
8	10	**AIN'T THAT A LOT OF LOVE** Simply Red (East West)	30345	1257	1375
9	22	**2 TIMES** Ann Lee (Systematic/London)	32391	909	1348
10	7	**SUMMER SON** Texas (Mercury)	21552	1321	1160
11	9	**SING IT BACK** Moloko (Echo)	27398	1286	1158
=12	14	**SUN IS SHINING** Bob Marley Vs Funkstar De Luxe (Club Tools/Edell)	29935	1193	1151
=12	17	**I'VE GOT YOU** Martine McCutcheon (Innocent)	17547	1066	1151
14	19	**I SAVED THE WORLD TODAY** Eurythmics (RCA)	26442	941	1139
15	21	**WHY DOES IT ALWAYS RAIN ON ME?** Travis (Independiente)	28897	922	1081
16	16	**WHEN YOU SAY NOTHING AT ALL** Ronan Keating (Polydor)	25969	1087	988
17	15	**MUCHO MAMBO** Shaft (Wonderboy)	25280	1188	951
18	13	**FRIENDS FOREVER** Thunderbugs (1st Avenue/Epic)	14619	1215	943
19	new	**SUNSHINE** Gabrielle (Go Beat)	21202	571	829
=20	24	**MY LOVE IS YOUR LOVE** Whitney Houston (Arista)	25165	794	787
=20	30	**SHE'S SO HIGH** Tal Bachman (Columbia)	19758	625	787
22	18	**LIVIN' LA VIDA LOCA** Ricky Martin (Columbia)	14111	1010	784
23	27	**NEVER LET YOU DOWN** Honeyz (1st Avenue/Mercury)	14359	660	756
24	25	**BEAUTIFUL STRANGER** Madonna (Maverick/Warner Bros.)	17678	766	738
25	20	**IF YOU HAD MY LOVE** Jennifer Lopez (Columbia)	15803	924	729
26	11	**MI CHICO LATINO** Geri Halliwell (EMI)	10954	1246	718
27	23	**BETTER OFF ALONE** DJ Jurgen Ps Alice Deejay (Positiva)	20651	906	700
28	new	**JESSE HOLD ON** B*Witched (Epic)	12185	555	683
29	26	**NOT OVER YOU YET** Diana Ross (EMI)	14457	732	669
30	12	**BAILAMOS** Enrique Iglesias (Interscope/Polydor)	11539	1235	623

© Music Control UK. Titles ranked by total number of plays on 46 mainstream independent local stations from 00.00 on Sun 3 Oct until 24.00 on Sat 9 Oct 1999
Source 3.18 (Music Week, 16 October 1999)

Pirate radio

Prior to Radio 1 starting in 1967, the BBC played only three to four hours of pop music a week! In the mid 1960s pirate radio stations operating offshore were being listened to by up to 2 million listeners. Stations such as Radio Caroline were simply broadcasting non-stop pop music, with a few adverts to earn revenue. Since 1973, independent local radio (ILR) stations have also been broadcasting music. However, despite a steady increase in the number of music radio stations, it is clear that many music fans – and indeed performers – are frustrated at the limited range of music broadcast. As a consequence, pirate radio continues to flourish, especially in the larger cities. With the advent of the Internet, other alternative means of distributing music have developed (see pages 66–7).

Source 3.19

What kinds of music tend to be ignored by commercial music stations and most of the Radio 1 programmes? Why do you think this is so?

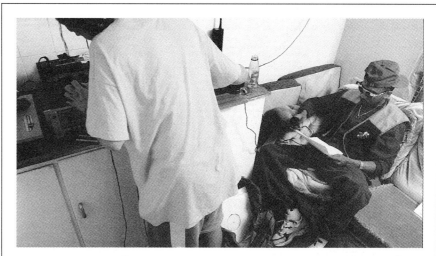

Out of concrete, jungle

The latest thing in rock reaches its fans via pirate broadcasters, operating from kitchens in tower blocks; Ben Thompson reports from the front line

Over the last two years, London's pirate music has changed, as music does. From hardcore – or to be more formal, Ardcore, a delirious twisted British derivative of American house music – it has mutated into jungle, an exclusively homegrown, London-based hybrid, incorporating elements of soul, hip-hop and especially ragga, whose overloading bass-lines and rumbling vocal style are ever more prominent.

As you listen to the pirate radio stations that have done so much to shape this music, the most notable feature is their inclusiveness. The voice of the DJ, or his mike-toting accomplice the MC (a double act which has its roots in the Jamaican dance halls of the Seventies), maps out a shifting pattern of greetings and affirmations: "Hold tight ... the man like John, the man like Chris ... hold tight the Dalston massive."

Nicky Blackmarket, who has been DJ-ing first on Pulse FM and now on Eruption 101.3 FM for more than three years, does not disagree. "It's very much a friendly thing – this is what

people on the outside don't understand. It's all about interacting with the listeners: they ring in and say 'nice show' or ask what clubs or raves the DJ is playing at, and we read their messages back to them off the pager.

"People that only hear about pirate radio on the news think that it's all drugs and violence, but it's nothing to do with that. We're not hurting anybody, we're not out mugging or murdering people. All we're doing illegally is broadcasting: giving people the chance to hear music which the major record companies and radio stations don't cater for."

Today's studio used to be someone's kitchen. Now the twin turntables and mixer unit sit on the draining board and the rhythms are cooking. There are council bin-liners on the windows and admonitory notes gaffer-taped to the walls: "Anyone who opens a window and disturbs the neighbours will be sacked": "Anyone caught leaving the studio and not cleaning up after them will lose their show."

Source 3.19 (*Independent on Sunday*, 17 July 1994)

Figure 3.10

**CASE STUDY:
EASTENDERS**

This chapter has been about the media as an **institution**. Having considered the influences on media production, such as ownership, the need for profit, the law, professional practice and so on, it is necessary to bring in the audience (discussed at length in Chapter 6). To answer the question posed at the beginning of the chapter – 'What brings producers and audiences together, and how is the relationship between them shaped?' – let us consider the case of a successful media product – the BBC's *EastEnders*.

Source 3.20 The development of *EastEnders*

1 From the description of *EastEnders*' development, draw a flow chart showing how each of the following influenced its rise to popularity:
   - the ratings;
   - the location;
   - the themes of the serial;
   - press reaction;
   - scheduling;
   - audience response.

2 Are there any recent developments that have affected the nature of the programme?

Source 3.20 (*BBC Research Findings, BBC 1986*)

EastEnders: the research contribution

On 19 February 1985 the BBC launched its new twice-weekly serial *EastEnders*. It was the BBC's first major soap opera since the 1960s ... The idea of producing a twice-weekly, year-round serial had originated in June 1981, and was promoted by an acute problem. BBC1's early evening weekday audience performance was poor. Instead of winning viewers in the early part of the evening who might stay with the channel for the rest of the night, BBC1's early evening audience fell off between 6.30 and 7.30pm ... Practical production considerations such as budgets, production teams, studios and so on determined that decisions on the fundamental basis for the serial, like where it would be located, were taken very early on in the planning stages ... Julia Smith had a clear idea of what she wanted to do but felt that her ideas would benefit from research and the views of the potential audience ... London emerged as an acceptable location, which coincided with the location Julia Smith had in mind: 'I knew all along what I really wanted to do, which was a series set in the East End of London. I'm a Londoner. All other soaps come from a different part of the country and I felt that the South was entitled to its own. I think the Cockneys have a vitality and a basic humour which is a necessary ingredient for a soap.' (Julia Smith, *The Times*, 1985).

In view of the 'dated' impressions of many other British soaps, potential viewers wanted the serial to address itself to current issues and concerns ...

February 1985: EastEnders goes on air

After a year of intense activity, amidst a blaze of publicity and considerable press and public scepticism, *EastEnders* went on air on 19 February 1985 at 7.00pm. It was dubbed by the press as 'the BBC's belated challenge to *Coronation Street* (Bhegani, *Time Out*, 1985) and by the public as 'Just another *Coronation Street* in the South' (*Group Discussions*, 1985). The BBC, however, hoped that by regularly scheduling it on Tuesdays and Thursdays at 7.00pm it would reverse the early evening dip in audience ratings ...

EastEnders started fairly strongly, the audience dipped during the spring and summer and from the autumn it started to build a loyal audience of its own, reaching an all-time high of 23 million over Christmas, less than a year after it was first shown ...

In common with other soaps *EastEnders* was initially most popular amongst women, older people and those in the working-class groups, but unusually for soaps it was not outstandingly more popular in the North than in the South. Unlike other soaps, after the first few tentative months the appeal of the serial extended across age groups and a year after it was launched *EastEnders* had the widest appeal of any soap opera on British television ...

By August is was improving on its share of viewers and was beginning to establish a following. Further steps were needed to consolidate and improve its position in the autumn, and these were taken when, as part of the new autumn schedules, *EastEnders* was rescheduled from 7.00pm to 7.30pm on Tuesdays and Thursdays.

Autumn 1985

The move to 7.30pm coincided with extensive media coverage of *EastEnders'* storylines, particularly in the 'whodunnit?' scandal surrounding schoolgirl Michelle Fowler's pregnancy. *EastEnders'* stories and its actors started to receive intense media interest ...

Increasingly numbers of viewers were making a conscious decision to make *EastEnders* a part of their regular weekly routine ... Viewers revealed that they now structured their lives around the programme, and that *EastEnders* had become a part of their social interaction. Viewers spoke about the characters as if they knew them well and elements of fact and fiction about the characters and actors had inevitably become blurred. The strengths of the serial were seen to lie in its confrontation of contemporary moral and social issues and its responsible treatment of 'delicate' subjects – the cot death and teenage pregnancy came in for special mention.

NEW TECHNOLOGY

Technological change is a constant feature of media production and consumption. Throughout the past century, new media technologies have developed with ever increasing rapidity. The past 25 years have seen the introduction of cable and satellite television, the video cassette recorder, video games consoles and the Walkman, to name but a few.

Without doubt, the most significant development in recent years has been the process of **digitalization**, whereby audiovisual and print output are communicated in digital form. This is the language of computers and it enables huge amounts of information (including pictures and sounds) to be stored and sent via fibre-optic cables or digital discs (for example, CD and videodisc). All media forms are being affected by digitalization, but the first to feel the full effects of the new technology were newspapers and magazines.

Desktop publishing (DTP)

Prior to the introduction of computers, newspaper and magazine production had remained unaltered for many decades. Journalists would type out stories, then these would be converted into lead type, page moulds and printing plates (the 'hot metal' process) that were then used to run off copies of the newspapers or magazines on printing presses.

Now, things are quite different. Stories and pictures are entered directly on to computers and publishing and graphics software is employed to create the pages on screen before these are sent electronically to laser printers or converted into plates for lithographic printing.

The main effects on newspapers have been:

- huge savings in production costs – for example, highly skilled printers are no longer needed;
- later deadlines;
- easier distribution – computerized page proofs can be sent on-line to printing centres.

Probably more important has been the effect desktop publishing has had on magazine production. For a modest outlay, it is possible to produce your own magazine (see the football fanzines on page 45). Indeed, some of the new magazines that have poured on to the market in recent years have progressed to high street newsagents (see Figures 3.14a and b).

the ZiNE

ISSUE 6 FEBRUARY 94 £1.65

Fascist brainwashing

Life at arse height

Ten steps to Stardom

Hetero'til proven queer

Get on a BTKA tape!

SEPULTURA

Wild Pumpkins at Midnight

PWEI

ZINE MARQUEE coupon

INTERNATIONAL   T SHIRT BARONS
PEEL HERE
Born To Kick Arse
LONDON
PEEL HERE

BTKA©

GO FOR IT - SHOW & SAY WHAT THE HELL YOU WANT IN THE ZiNE

...ems, scripts, ideas, letters, personal thoughts, free ads, ANYTHING !

Figure 3.11a

Talkin' 'bout their generation

How can Zine beat the youth culture trap?   **Alex Spillius**

An old farmhouse in deepest Surrey might seem the last place you would expect to find one of the country's fastest-growing youth magazines. But the very success of Zine has been a great surprise. It went from nought to 60,000 copies in six months. The April issue is the second monthly, after five issues in six-week cycles beginning in July. It is the first full-scale national fanzine, and as such the first national magazine entirely made up of readers' contributions.

More than 100 contributors gave something to the current issue, whether words, photographs, cartoons or illustrations. There are numerous band reviews, letters, rages against the establishment, and surreal illustrations, but the personal stories and poems are most striking. A converted ecstasy freak warns of the drug's dangers, a teenager tells how she was abused by her best female friend, an adolescent gay relates his suicide attempt.

Editor Bo Maggs resents the youth-magazine label, but the crammed, multi-layered design, and the indie music content, would keep most 26-pluses away, while the vast majority of contributors appear to be under 25.

With no previous experience save for a computer graphics course, designer Cedric Peate now designs and makes up the 100-page magazine on an Apple Mac 2CI and 2FX using Quark Xpress and Aldus Freehand.

Figure 3.11b (*The Guardian*, 4 April 1994)

Six steps to becoming a magazine mogul

1. You will need an AppleMac and someone who can use it to design your layouts and give the magazine some style and identity. You also need a phone and lots of willing friends. *Blow* magazine, however, gets by with a photocopier.

2. Get cash. Tom Hodgkinson, editor of *The Idler*, says that about £800 is enough if you are going to start off with a modest 1,000 issues. He recommends getting friends and family to invest sums of £50 or £100.

3. Now you need a printer. Shop around, look at which companies print other independent small-run magazines that you like. Bargain. Many printers are willing to do deals for cash and further concessions for new projects if they look like a long-term winner.

4. Distribution is the next problem. Places like the ICA, Tower Records and shops like American Retro, will take magazines from you directly on a sale or return basis. But if you are printing over 1,000 copies then you will have to go to magazine wholesalers which can be difficult as they often only deal with one part of London or the country. The other choice is to sign up with a magazine distributor which will deal with all the wholesalers for you. Bad news is that they take about 55 per cent of your cover price and pay half of this money after 45 days, the remainder after 120 days. This makes cash-flow a nightmare after issue one.

5. Get more money. Unless you want to be a quarterly magazine, you're going to have to think up something quick. This can be partially solved by selling subscriptions which give you a much higher return or organising parties and club events; *aBeSea* holds a launch party for each issue: you get into the bash by buying a copy at the door. But the answer is advertising.

6. Get selling advertising space which clients have to pay for within days of the magazine coming out. All this cash is for you. No worries. You are on your way.

Figure 3.12 (*Time Out*, 2–9 March 1994)

Cable and satellite television

Satellite television was launched in Europe in 1982, while broadband cable (using optical fibres) was introduced to Britain in 1984. The progress of both satellite and cable has been slow and steady. Satellite television grew most rapidly in the 1990s, largely due to its being more accessible than cable in many areas, and the acquisition of Premier League football rights in 1992.

By 1995, over 4 million homes had signed up for satellite and cable television, and by 1999 this figure had topped 7 million, though this is still well below half of the British viewing population. This is in spite of the fact that dozens of extra channels are available, and many sporting events and new films are exclusive to satellite and cable subscribers.

Source 3.21

What does the table reveal about the impact of new satellite and cable channels on overall television viewing?

Three companies (Telewest, NTL and Cable & Wireless) own the vast majority of cable franchises in Britain. Telewest is part-owned by Microsoft – the richest company in the world.

Choice and access

Do more channels mean more choice?

ACTIVITY

Examine what channels are available on satellite and cable. Which particular types of programmes are most commonly offered? Are there any examples of channels offering programme types or choices not available on the five terrestrial channels?

Cable television has the ability to offer community channels that enable the local population to receive programmes about their own area. In some cases, it provides access to ordinary people to participate in programme making. This is an example of **narrowcast** television, where specialist or minority audiences are supplied with programmes tailored to their interests.

However, the opportunity to enjoy the full range of additional channels provided by cable and satellite television is restricted primarily by your ability to pay. Whereas the terrestrial channels may be viewed once the licence fee has been paid, cable and satellite are only available to those paying monthly subscription fees. In addition, many individual programmes – such as boxing matches or newly released films – can only be watched on a pay per view basis. The consequence of this is to deny access to some popular programmes or sports coverage that were once 'freely' available to everyone.

A final issue is that of whether or not the success of cable and satellite television may seriously weaken the BBC and ITV's services because of smaller audiences and declining revenue.

ANNUAL PERCENTAGE SHARES OF VIEWING (INDIVIDUALS) (1981–1997)

	BBC1	BBC2	ITV (inc.GMTV)	CH4	CH5	OTHERS (Cable/Sat/RTE)
1981	39	12	47	–	–	–
1983	37	11	48	4	–	–
1985	36	11	46	7	–	–
1987	38	12	42	8	–	–
1989	39	11	42	9	–	–
1991	34	10	42	10	–	4
1992	34	10	41	10	–	5
1993	33	10	40	11	–	6
1994	32	11	39	11	–	7
1995	32	11	37	11	–	9
1996	33	12	35	11	–	10
1997	31	12	33	11	3	12
1998	30	11	32	10	4	13

Source 3.21 (BARB, 1999)

Digital television

Until 1998, all television output was restricted by limited broadcasting bandwidth. This is the 'space' available for carrying the transmitter signals sent by different television companies. Hence, Britain has had only four (and in 1997 a fifth) national channels available to viewers. Digitalization means that:

- many more channels can be fitted into the same broadcasting space;
- picture and sound quality are improved;
- information may be sent both ways between the television provider and viewer (via phone lines).

In 1998, BSkyB launched its digital service, quickly followed by On Digital. Both services require a set-top box (decoder) to convert the digital signals, enabling viewers to receive over 50 channels and an electronic programme guide to 'navigate' through the channels. In 1999, cable began to offer its digital services (see Figure 3.16), which, because it is delivered by phone lines with huge capacity for carrying audio-visual data, offers the greatest potential for **interactivity**.

Interactive television means viewers can exercise considerably more choice in terms of how and what they view on television. This includes options such as:

- selecting different camera shots for viewing live sports;
- participating in live television programmes such as quiz shows, debates and so on;
- home shopping, banking and other such services;
- playing video games;
- e-mail and the Internet.

It seems likely that digital television will prove to be successful because of two factors. First, the cost to customers of setting themselves up to receive the services (primarily the set-top boxes, dish, installation and so on) has been heavily subsidized. Despite costing several hundred pounds to manufacture, the equipment required has been supplied free to households. Second, the government has announced that, eventually (about 2010), existing analogue television services will be switched off.

Nevertheless, history shows that developments in television technology often take a considerable time before being fully adopted by the vast majority of the population (see Figure 3.17).

Active Digital is more than just TV and phone

What else?

Right now, in addition to multi-channel TV and savings on your phone, just one Active Digital connection can bring you Digital Internet, a fast and reliable link to the information and entertainment riches of the World Wide Web.
All you need are a compatible computer and a modem.

And the future?

Soon, you can look forward to unlocking the full promise of Active Digital with ultra-fast Internet access, interactive video games, on-line shopping and banking, Videophone and much much more. You'll be at the hub of a global system, providing you with a whole host of new services that will entertain you better, inform you more thoroughly, let you communicate more effectively and help you to manage your life.

Figure 3.13 *Telewest Cable*

Figure 3.14 (*Broadcast*, 9 January 1998)

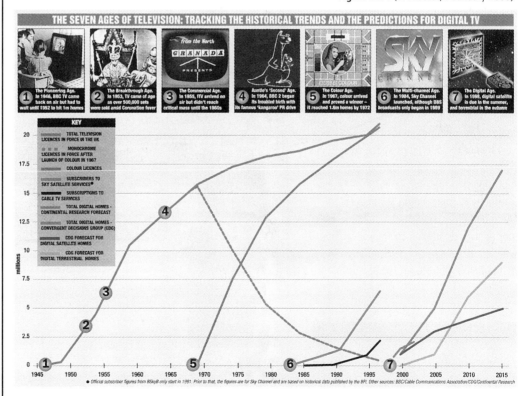

The Internet

This contains the World Wide Web, which consists of millions of pages of information stored on computer networks around the world. These pages may feature printed text, pictures, music – in fact, the full range of content found in the everyday media, including newspapers, magazines, radio stations and music concerts. As computer capacity grows, then film and television programmes will also become available. In 1999, the first live football match – England v. Scotland – was transmitted live on the Internet.

The Internet is a rapidly growing medium, expanding globally by about 100,000 each day. It is truly heralding a communications revolution affecting all media forms to some degree.

Newspapers

It is now possible to keep up to date with news developments by logging on to a range of websites that provide continual news services. While newspapers will not be replaced by the Internet (they are cheap, portable and easier on the eye), they are having to adapt their own products for on-line usage. The advantages for the newspaper include more space to develop features, up-to-the-minute reporting and the possibility of interactivity (responding to readers). More generally, the Internet means stories may be broken by non-newspaper sources. However, the problem here is in distinguishing fact from rumour or gossip.

ACTIVITY

Visit a newspaper on the Internet (the website addresses are usually printed on the front page) and see how the on-line version differs from the printed one.

Television

While television companies such as the BBC have developed very informative websites, they do not broadcast programmes on the Internet. Instead, it is currently left to 'amateurs' to broadcast, or **webcast**, their programmes. Much of this output is based on continuous live video input from a camcorder (**webcam**). Outside webcasts feature street scenes, nature and weather watches while indoor webcasts include nightclubs (cyber-clubbing), shops or even bedrooms!

Magazines

As with newspapers, most magazines have developed on-line editions. The real potential for **webzines** lies in the ability of any individual or group to devise a website that caters for a specialist interest or activity that is ignored by the magazine market (see Figure 3.18, an example of a television programme website, including Flat Eric – a character from a Levis advertising campaign of 1999). This is similar to fanzines (see pages 61–3), but allows far more regular updates and reader participation.

Music

As the Internet is a digital medium, it has the capacity to deliver CD-quality sound. With the addition of an MP3 player (which compresses the sound files so they can be easily downloaded), music can be transmitted over the Internet into people's homes virtually free of charge. The music industry faces a twin threat. First, there is piracy – it is difficult to prevent people feeding music on to a website for others to download. Second, performers now have the option to bypass the major music companies and distribute their music on-line.

Source 3.22

In what ways might the Internet change the way music is consumed?

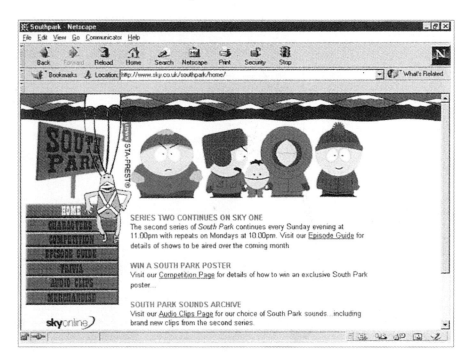

Figure 3.15

CHUCK IT ON THE NET

Public Enemy are taking on the record companies and releasing their new album on the web. Randeep Ramesh meets Chuck D, the force behind the revolution.

Chuck D has spent most of his artistic life proclaiming revolutions – now hip-hop's most articulate voice is leading one. The front man of Public Enemy believes the release of the band's latest record, There's A Poison Going On, will irrevocably change the face of the music industry. For Public Enemy have become the first mainstream group to release an album on-line. Although the latest slab of the group's rhetoric will hit these shores in shrink-wrapped plastic later this month, There's A Poison Going On can already be downloaded from a website (www.atomicpop.com) for just £6.

'We are going to drag the major labels into the 21st century kicking and screaming,' intones the rapper.

Chuck D's public spat with his label, Def Jam, ended their 12-year association – a shock for anyone who has heard the rapper repeatedly praise the company in verse. Instead, the hip-hop collective have opted for the virtual world. Earlier this year, Public Enemy launched a digital radio station on the Internet (www.bringthenoise.com) and now offer free video clips from their latest tour on their 'home' site.

Source 3.22 (*The Guardian*, 18 June 1999)

Future developments

As media technologies are all moving towards digitally stored information, then there is an ever-increasing trend towards **media convergence**. This means that each media source may act as a supplier of several forms of information and entertainment. Initially the television set-top box is at the forefront of this trend, but, in the near future, the following developments seem likely:

- the Internet being available on television, games consoles and mobile phones;
- the television set and/or computer screen offering the full range of media services – television, film, shopping, music and so on;
- the personalization of media supply and individuals being able to choose media output designed especially for their individual tastes.

What is not known is which particular media form or application will dominate. Whether digital television, PCs or the Internet will triumph is uncertain.

The key questions

- *Cost*
  What effect will the cost of new technologies have on both producers and audiences? Will there be an increasing division between those who can and cannot afford access to the new media?

- *Audience needs*
  How far will the new technologies meet audience needs? For every successful new media development, there are several failures, especially where there are competing formats (VHS v. Betamax video, Sega v. Nintendo v. Sony games consoles and others).

- *Regulation*
  How far will governments allow new media technology to go unregulated? Will governments be able to control what appears in new media, such as the Internet? Will the market become dominated by a few all-powerful global companies?

How the giants line up

Merger draws on AOL's net presence and Time Warner's sprawling media empire

Wonder of the web

AOL.COM

NEW! - My AOL.COM: Now You Can Customize
News, Weather, Stocks & More.

► AOL Mail ► My AOL.COM ► People/Chat ► Search ► Shop ► Web Centers ► Try AOL FREE!

AOL Anytime, Anywhere

Wednesday, January 12, 2000

Daily Essentials

Check Your AOL Mail

TOP NEWS:

AOL is the internet's leading service provider, reaching more than 20 million members

Net's global reach

Canada owns 20% of ISP

US largest service provider with 20m customers

AOL Europe 50/50 joint venture with Bertelsmann – operates in nine countries and four languages

AOL UK and France partnership

AOL Japan

Hong Kong AOL Chinese language service launched 1999

AOL Latin America 50/50 joint venture

AOL Brazil

AOL Mexico and Argentina to come

Australia AOL has 50/50 joint venture with Bertelsmann

Warner's Matrix

Time Warner: Big is beautiful

Broadcasting
More than 1bn viewers
CNN
HBO
Cartoon network

CNN

TV production
Hits include:
The Sopranos
ER
Sex in the City

Music
Five labels
Stars on the roster include:
Madonna
Seal
Cher
Brandy
Tori Amos
Jewel
Busta Rhymes
Morcheeba
Phil Collins

Magazines
32 titles, with 120m readers
Time
People
Sports Illustrated
Fortune
Life
Wallpaper
Book sales topped $1bn in 1998

Film production
Warner Bros.
Eyes Wide Shut
The Matrix
LA Confidential
Wild Wild West
New Line Cinema
Rush Hour
Austin Powers

Madonna

ER: Geeorge Clooney

Figure 3.16 (*AOL/Time Warner* merger)

Because the Internet has the ability to supply all forms of media content, it is not surprising that large media corporations have begun to form relationships with Internet servers (the companies that allow people to access the Internet). The first example of such a merger occurred in January 2000 when the world's largest media corporation, Time Warner, was taken over by AOL, the world's largest Internet server (see Figure 3.16). This will mean AOL subscribers will have priority access to all of Time Warner's media content.

4 REPRESENTATION

1 It is often said that television is a 'window on the world'. What do you think is meant by this statement?

2 How is looking at the world through a television screen different from looking at the world through a window in your house or classroom?

It is not possible for the media to present the world as it really is (see pages 15–21). Because the media construct reality, they change or **mediate** what is really there. To mediate means to come between, and thereby to change or represent. Although much work goes into producing a natural 'this is the way the world is' picture of events, places, people, and so on, it can never be pure or exact. This does not mean media professionals deliberately set out to misrepresent things, but simply that the printed word, the photograph, television picture, or whatever all involve choices. It is always necessary to select and thus provide a particular way of seeing something. The news is a good example (see pages 52–4), but it applies equally to entertainment. The questions are what ideas, beliefs and attitudes are represented in the media?

Figure 4.1

STEREOTYPING

Stereotyping is labelling a whole group in a certain way, usually unfairly. For example, a stereotyped belief about people who live in the country is that they are old-fashioned, suspicious of strangers and rather simple.

ACTIVITY

Try to list as many stereotypes of groups as possible. How do you think these stereotypes have developed?

It is not easy to avoid using stereotypes. It enables us to generalize about people of whom we might not know very much. Teachers are as guilty of this as anyone, labelling pupils as stupid, hard-working, lazy and so on. However, when one group stereotypes another it is often with the intention of controlling them. The result may be domination, exploitation and even violence. For example, Hitler promoted very strong anti-Jewish stereotyping in the 1930s, which led eventually to Jews being murdered in concentration camps.

Stereotyping and media representations

Representing groups in the media often involves stereotyping. There are even stereotypes of those working in the media, such as football commentators, DJs, tabloid journalists and others.

Source 4.1

1 Which stereotypes are represented in these pictures?
2 How might stereotypes help in achieving large audiences?
3 In which parts of the media are stereotypes most likely to be used?

It is important to recognize that there is often significant variation within a broad stereotype. For example, many soap operas contain a neighbourhood gossip or local rogue, but these stereotypes become **individuated** as the characters develop over time.

Source 4.1

GENDER REPRESENTATIONS

Males and females are often represented differently in the media.

Sources 4.2 a and b

1 How are masculinity and femininity signified in these adverts?
2 What do the terms 'masculine' and 'feminine' mean? Compare your answers with those of other members of your class.

Teenage magazines

While there are many magazines and comics explicitly produced for girls, there are few clearly aimed at boys.

Sources 4.3 a and b

1 Compare and contrast these pages from *Bliss* and *Match* with respect to the:
   - type of information provided;
   - choice of images and language;
   - layout and design;
   - any other differences.

2 Why do you think there are no boys' magazines equivalent to *Bliss*?

Source 4.2a

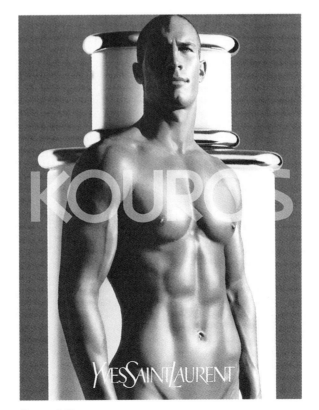

Source 4.2b

Source 4.3a (*Bliss*, September 1998)

Source 4.3b (*Match*, 31 July 1999)

Content analysis

This is a method of trying to discover whether or not there are any patterns or common features appearing in media content. After selecting suitable category headings, an attempt is made to count the number of examples appearing in the media (in adverts, television fiction, newspaper stories and so on).

Source 4.4

How might the patterns in this table be explained?

Frequency of women and men by type of programme				
	Men	Women	Men %	Women %	Approx. ratio of men:women
National news	819	184	82	18	4:1
Factual	1011	489	67	33	2:1
Light entertainment	478	203	70	30	7:3
Sport	145	13	92	8	11:1
Religious	5	4	56	44	3:2
Children's programmes	25	22	53	47	1:1
Fiction	597	402	60	40	3:2
Film	409	176	70	30	7:3
Totals	3489	1493	70	30	7:3

Source 4.4 (Broadcasting Standards Council, *Perspectives of Women in Television, 1994)*

ACTIVITY

Select ten adverts containing male and female subjects. From the adverts, identify the following:

1 How many males and females appear?
2 What is their approximate age and physical appearance?
3 What roles/status are represented – job or activity; single or married?
4 How are the people portrayed (for example, funny, active)?
5 Where do they appear – what is the setting (for example, the home)?
6 What sex is used for the voice-over?

From your findings (rough notes) produce a table that summarizes the results.

Write an analysis of the main conclusions.

- Are there any clear patterns?
- Are there any surprising results?
- Were the adverts easy to categorize?

Gender and physical representation

In modern society, it is still common to find that females are more often judged by their physical appearance than other qualities they may possess. Beauty contests typify this attitude. Although the BBC no longer cover the Miss World contest, much of the media still place a great emphasis on a woman's looks, e.g. page 3 of *The Sun* and other papers.

Source 4.5a

Sources 4.5 a and b

1 Why have women's bodies been used in these adverts?

2 Why do you think male bodies are rarely used in adverts other than with products for the body such as clothes and aftershave?

PILKINGTON MAKES OVER 20% OF THE WORLD'S FLAT GLASS. SOMETHING THAT'S EASILY IGNORED.

Source 4.5b

amaaaazing!

XR-M28 Micro Hi-Fi System

beautifully proportioned
deceptively powerful
seductively small
a great looker
unbeatable value for money
in a word...

aiwa

For our latest catalogue and details of your local dealer, call our Customer Information Centre on 0990 902 902 (all calls charged at national rate) http://www.aiwa.co.uk
● HI-FI SYSTEMS ● PERSONAL MINI-DISC ● VIDEOS ● TV'S ● PERSONAL STEREOS ● PORTABLE AUDIO ● ACCESSORIES ● IN-CAR AUDIO

Source 4.6 (*TV Times*, 14 November 1987)

With a bubbly personality and striking looks to match, *Emmerdale Farm* actress Malandra Burrows – pictured right with Ian Sharrock, who plays Jackie Merrick – should have no problem attracting boyfriends in real life. But Malandra is finding just the opposite applies. As Woolpack barmaid Kathy Bates she is getting engaged to Jackie Merrick this week, and the happy couple are featured on our cover and overpage.

But the blonde, blue-eyed actress, who was 22 earlier this month, confesses that her hectic life revolves around the ITV serial and leaves little time for off-screen romance. 'I have to admit that becoming engaged to Jackie Merrick this week is some compensation,' she says.

The problem is not a lack of boyfriends but her busy rehearsal and filming schedule, combined with the public attention that a regular screen role brings. 'It's a

Pulling pints – but not men

question of having the time to let a relationship develop,' says Malandra.

'And when people come up to me because they recognise me from *Emmerdale*, I enjoy it. But boyfriends have found it difficult to cope with this situation because of the pressure it imposes.

'At the moment, there is no one special in my life, but I have so little time that I can rarely manage even to get back home to see the family in Liverpool. Still, I'm not complaining, especially as I am enjoying *Emmerdale* so much and my role is opening up. If Jackie Merrick and I do marry, you can bet it won't all be plain-sailing.'

Malandra is still staying in the same Yorkshire bed-and-breakfast house near the television studios that she started using more than two years ago.

'Living out of a suitcase doesn't get me down,' she says. 'In fact, I get spoilt rotten by the landlady.'

Source 4.6

1 In what terms is actress Malandra Burrows described in the *TV Times* profile?

2 If the profile had been of Ian Sharrock, the male character, what terms might have been used to describe him?

3 Turn to source 2.7a on page 17. Why do you think *The Sun* has focused on the woman rather than the man in the story?

Turn to source 2.7a on page 17.

ACTIVITY

Watch the television news and weather forecasts for a week on all the channels, and describe the male and female presenters in terms of their age and physical appearance. Do there seem to be any significant differences based on the gender of the presenters?

CASE STUDY: GENDER AND SPORT

Despite high levels of participation in both the playing and watching of sport by women, media coverage of sport in Britain tends to be from a male perspective. In practice, this means two things. First, sportswomen are virtually ignored by the media. This is borne out by a three-month survey of television and national newspaper coverage of sport during spring 1998 (conducted by Nottingham Trent University). For example, only 0.5 per cent of all sports stories in *The Sun* featured women. While the BBC did devote some time to women's sports, it still amounted to only just over a fifth of all sports coverage. Further evidence is provided by the 1999 Women's Football World Cup in the USA. Although the tournament was extensively covered in many countries (including the USA where football is not a national sport), it was virtually ignored by the British media.

ACTIVITY

Conduct a survey into the amount of media sports coverage by doing the following.

1 Collect copies of a tabloid and a broadsheet newspaper for a week and measure the numbers of column inches and pictures devoted to men's and women's sport respectively.

2 Record all sports programmes on BBC1 and ITV during a week and count the hours and minutes each channel devotes to men's and women's sport.

Source 4.7 a and b

What do these sources suggest about the seriousness with which the Women's tennis is being tested?

Source 4.7a (*The Sun*, 22 June 1999)

Kourn's in good shape
By STEVEN HOWARD

RELAX, boys, the luscious Anna Kournikova is still on the prowl at Wimbledon.

Kournikova – aka Pornikova (on the WTA circuit), Superbabe and Babushka – lives to fight another day.

But the 18 year old with the looks that could stop a 93 bus in its tracks on Wimbledon Common was pushed all the way by 5ft 11in, 10st 12lb Austrian Barbara Schwartz. It was no doodle against the Strudel for 17th seed Kournikova, who needed 1hr 43min to see off hard-hitting Schwartz 7–6 4–6 6–2.

Anna, a semi-finalist at her only Wimbledon two years ago, said: 'It was a tough match but the most important thing is to survive these early rounds.

'I'm playing well, feeling well and even serving well – I got seven aces in today.'

Laughing

But when it came to more important matters — like her 'romance' with Ronaldo — she was NOT coming up with the goods.

Laughing if off, she said: 'The last time I saw Ronaldo was the only time I saw him – at the French Open.'

It took all Kournikova's versatility on grass to beat Schwartz, 19.

But the boys – young, middle-aged, old and even older – found Court No2 an irresistible attraction.

And no one was disagreeing when Anna said: 'I'm in pretty good shape all round.'

... The Russian teenager Anna Kournikova was on TV. She lost her match but the men crowded around the TV here in the sports room weren't particularly bothered by that. Miss Kournikova is quite simply a stunning-looking girl and every national newspaper has needed little excuse to run big pictures of her ...

Presenter to Sunday Mail's Chief Sports Writer:

You are one of the few journalists to have had a close encounter with her.

Sports Writer:

Yes; she was being introduced as the face of the millennium for a sports bra.

Presenter:

A sports bra? It gets better all the time. Keep on talking!

Source **4.7b** *Papertalk*, Radio 5, 18th June 1999

Source 4.8

How would male audiences react to this kind of treatment of sportsmen by female commentators?

Source **4.8** (*Independent on Sunday*, 27 June 1999)

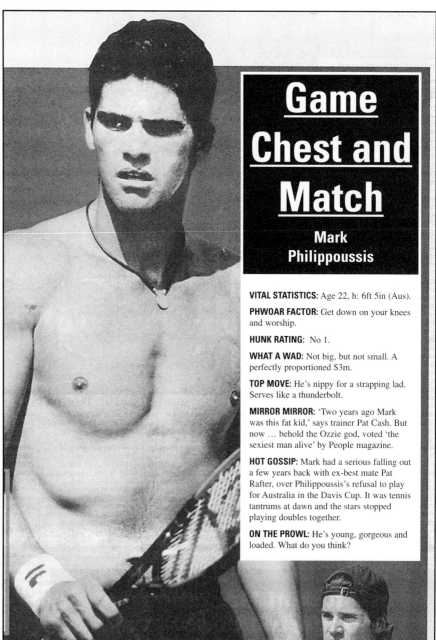

Game Chest and Match

Mark Philippoussis

VITAL STATISTICS: Age 22, h: 6ft 5in (Aus).

PHWOAR FACTOR: Get down on your knees and worship.

HUNK RATING: No 1.

WHAT A WAD: Not big, but not small. A perfectly proportioned $3m.

TOP MOVE: He's nippy for a strapping lad. Serves like a thunderbolt.

MIRROR MIRROR: 'Two years ago Mark was this fat kid,' says trainer Pat Cash. But now ... behold the Ozzie god, voted 'the sexiest man alive' by People magazine.

HOT GOSSIP: Mark had a serious falling out a few years back with ex-best mate Pat Rafter, over Philippoussis's refusal to play for Australia in the Davis Cup. It was tennis tantrums at dawn and the stars stopped playing doubles together.

ON THE PROWL: He's young, gorgeous and loaded. What do you think?

Changing representations of gender

Women's magazines

Women's magazines have undergone several changes since the war. Marjorie Ferguson examined how they had changed between 1949 and 1974 in *Forever Feminine*. She found that the main theme in the 1950s weeklies was 'getting and keeping your man', especially in the short stories. Gradually, the theme of 'self-help' appeared – either in the form of being a better mother, lover, worker, cook and so on, or by overcoming misfortune, such as divorce or illness.

By the mid 1970s, women doing paid work outside the home had become a major concern. Magazines such as *Cosmopolitan* were promoting the role of 'independent women', capable of earning their own living, and being sexually adventurous. However, Marjorie Ferguson found that, throughout the period, the magazines still concentrated on 'him, home and looking good'.

During the 1980s and 1990s, there has been a large increase in the number of magazines targeting female readers. For younger readers, there has been a shift away from the emphasis on idealized romance and towards a more realistic representation of relationships with men (See the *Minx* front cover on page 121). More generally, many of the magazines, such as *More* and *New Woman*, reflect women's greater sexual assertiveness. Whether they actively encourage or celebrate women's independence (especially from domestic responsibilities) is open to question. Many critics of women's magazines argue that they still restrict women's horizons by emphasizing being successful in personal relationships (especially with men).

Sources 4.9 a and b

How do these extracts from a 1958 issue of *Woman's Realm* contrast with the content of such magazines today? Try to use *Woman*, *Woman's Realm* or *Woman's Own* as a comparison.

Something to *talk about*
by Vera Wynn Griffiths

Esmé had always longed to be the stay-at-home wife; but leisure had unexpected disadvantages

Esmé went out to the car to see David off to work.

'D'you know, this is the first time I've really felt like your wife,' she said excitedly.

'I must say I like that!' he said with a grin, 'considering you've been my wife for three years now.'

'Oh, I know, but – it's just – well never mind, it would take too long to explain now. Goodbye, come home early.'

She stood waving until the car was round the corner, then turned back indoors, into the kitchen where the breakfast dishes were stacked. After washing up, she thought she'd turn out the spare bedroom and wash the curtains; then she'd make a ginger cake. David loved ginger cake and there hadn't been time to make one lately; and some time this morning she'd have to look at her cacti which she kept in the little glass-fronted porch.

The day stretched before her in long, blissful emptiness. There was time for everything now. This afternoon she'd go into town and do some shopping; not hurried shopping for two chops and the necessary groceries, but the sort of shopping when you pottered about looking into windows, drifting into the market, really choosing food. And tonight supper wouldn't be cold ham and a tomato and a bite of cheese. She'd make a bacon and egg pie and a lemon soufflé to follow ...

The clock chimed half-past eight and here she was still in an apron and slippers. On every other weekday morning during her three years of marriage, she had been properly dressed by this time; face done, hair done, tearing down the road to catch the bus which would take her to the school. That was what she'd meant when she told David that for the first time she felt like his wife. This was the very first morning that she'd been able to stand on the doorstep and wave him off. Always until now, there had been that ghastly rush, both of them getting ready, swallowing some breakfast, trying to get the dishes done so that they wouldn't be there facing them in the evening.

Source 4.9a (*Woman's Realm*, 1958)

May I help you?

asks Clare Shepherd

If you want a reply by post, please enclose a 3d. stamp. Address your letters to Clare Shepherd, Woman's Realm, 189 High Holborn, London, W.C.1. You can be sure that letters either for publication or to be answered privately will be treated confidentially, and that your identity will not be disclosed.

Q My sister, who is about five years older than me, has been engaged to a very charming young man for the past three years. They want to get married, but they cannot find anywhere to live.

I am very fond of my sister's fiancé, who has always acted like a brother to me, but recently his behaviour has changed, and he has tried flirting with me. Once or twice he has even kissed me rather passionately.

I don't want to hurt my sister by telling her this, but I do want to stop this kind of behaviour. What do you suggest?

A The best thing to do is to see as little of this young man as you can manage without comment. Don't change so markedly as to arouse suspicion in your sister's mind. Also tell the young man that you are certainly not going to betray your sister.

I expect the long engagement has proved trying for both of them and the sooner they can be married the better. In the meantime, I am glad to find that you are being sensible, and not taking this young man's flirtation seriously. You yourself, I feel, should be getting out more, and meeting young folk of both sexes.

Q My girl has told me she never wants to see me again. We had been going steady for six months, and we planned to be married. Then she began to grow distant, and we had our first quarrel when she told me she didn't want me to take her home to her digs. I love her as much as ever.

Yesterday I waited for her on her way to the office, but, as soon as she saw me, she crossed the road. I went over to speak to her, and we had a dreadful scene right there in the street. I cannot understand why she has changed so.

A You know better than I can whether there was any reason for this change in your fiancée. As you say that your first quarrel arose from her refusal to let you take her home, I am wondering whether you perhaps forced physical attentions on her when she was not ready for them, perhaps when you were wishing her good night. Of course, I may be quite wrong in this assumption, but the more you love your girl the stronger will be your desire for physical expression. This is natural and is nothing to be ashamed of – but all the same, you are the person who should protect your girl from doing anything she may regret. She may just have found that she does not love you as much as she thought she did. If this is the case, I am afraid you will just have to grin and bear it. You are not the first person who has loved in vain and it is far better that your girl should find she has made a mistake before marriage rather than after. She is within her rights in refusing to have anything more to do with you and you should accept this and avoid any further scenes. If this behaviour is just a tantrum, she is far more likely to come back to you if you respect her wishes now.

Q Most parents seem to worry when their teenage children begin to take an interest in the opposite sex. My problem is just the opposite. I have a daughter of sixteen who is still at school. She is very intelligent and her teacher thinks she may get a scholarship for further study.

Her father and I are pleased about this, but I am worried about her because she seems to be far too serious for her age. She has no close friends and takes no interest in boys. Am I worrying unnecessarily?

A It is rather unusual for a girl of sixteen to show no interest in boys, but don't forget that some girls develop later than others, and that there is no way you can force her interest.

You could try to make her more sociable by encouraging her to bring friends home. If she has a room of her own, you might help her to entertain her friends in it by turning it into a bed-sitter, and encouraging her to give tea or light supper parties. Adolescents of your daughter's age are often shy of meeting their friends in the company of their parents. If this plan works, you might then suggest a party with boys among the guests. All that will be necessary will be a gramophone and a few rock 'n' roll records, a room to dance in, and some light refreshments. Though you may not care for rock 'n' roll, it does take the starch out of boys and girls who are otherwise inclined to be stand-offish and shy.

Finally, do make sure that your daughter has some becoming clothes, good hair-style – and as a special present why not let her have a lesson in make-up.

Source 4.9b (*Woman's Realm*, 1958)

Sources 4.10a and b

What ideas about women and work do these two adverts represent?

Mens Magazines

The 1990s has seen a huge increase in the circulation of magazines aimed at male readers. For example, *FHM* rose from 50,000 copies sold each month in 1994 to over 600,000 monthly circulation by 1998 (outselling all the women's monthly titles). This sudden rise in popularity was sparked by the success of *Loaded*, launched in 1994 with the catchphrase 'For men who should know better'. This was a reference to the magazines' pandering to readers who enjoyed the more traditional male interests, such as football, alcohol, looking at scantily clad women and generally 'having a laugh'. Magazines such as *FHM* and *Loaded* have been called 'lads magazines', and their success has led to the launch of many similar titles as well as a change in policy for those male magazines such as *GQ* and *Esquire* that had been focusing more on fashion and self-improvement. The most obvious change was the replacement of male images on the magazine covers by images of young, sexually suggestive women (or 'babes').

Source 4.11

What kind of masculine identity and lifestyle seems to be represented by this first issue of *Front*?

Source 4.11

Source 4.10a

Source 4.10b

Television

While in some television genres, such as soap opera, there has long been a tradition of having strong independent female characters, it is only in recent years that women have begun to feature in what are often thought to be 'masculine' genres. For example, following the pioneering 1980s American police series *Cagney and Lacey*, there has been a growing number of British television police series having leading female characters, such as *Prime Suspect* and *The Cops* (see page 110).

Source 4.12

1 To what extent is Jaye Griffiths' character in *The Bill* an example of a 'token' black female succeeding in an area of masculine domination on television?
2 How important is it for such female characters to be physically attractive?

Few areas of television are now exclusively masculine. Even sports programmes include female presenters, such as Sue Barker (*A Question of Sport*), and within television drama, there is the example of *Playing the Field* revolving around a women's football team. Meanwhile, American television has seen the rise of a number of comedy/drama series based on working women.

Source 4.13

How far do series such as *Ally McBeal* seem to offer a genuinely new representation of women's lives?

ACTIVITY

Compare the representations of young single women with that of men in situation comedies such as *Men Behaving Badly* or *Friends*.

Ever since she walked into Sun Hill nick four months ago to take over from Burnside, Detective Inspector Sally Johnson has had to put up with hurtful jibes and sexist remarks.

Okay, she's a woman and she's black. But *The Bill's* new CID boss is no token. After 11 years in the force, she's got where she is by being tough, dedicated and determined not to put up with any nonsense. And the boys at Sun Hill had better believe it's wise not to mess with their new skipper.

Sally's like steel. She's heard it all before and there's no way she's going to be needled. Even so, Jaye Griffiths, who plays TV's most senior black woman detective, reckons her battle to break through deeply held prejudices is far from over.

'Sally's always going to have to fight her corner,' she says. 'When she first arrived she waded in a bit like a bull in a china shop because she knew she'd be facing a lot of hostility.' But the resentment some of them feel at taking orders from her is not about to disappear overnight.

Her sparring with Inspector Monroe has less to do with prejudice than rivalry between two equally-ranked officers. And so far there's been no real resentment from the more junior Det Sgt Greig. But that doesn't mean she's been fully accepted.

'Sally feels the pain of hurtful remarks but after so many years working her way up the ranks she can see them coming a mile off,' says Jaye. 'To her, they're boring because they're so predictable.

'I don't think its any easier for someone like Sally to achieve promotion in the police now – what's easier is dealing with the nonsense. If a remark is made to her that's out of order, there are boards she can approach to make a formal complaint.'

'I won't be pushed around'
says Sun Hill's Sally

As The Bill's tough and ambitious new Detective Inspector, Jaye Griffiths is really laying down the law

'Sally's always going to have to fight her corner,' says Jaye, above right with DC Skase (Iain Fletcher) and DS Pearce (Martin Marquez)

Picture by Alan Olley/Scope

6 TVTimes

Source 4.12 (*TV Times*, 9–15 April 1994)

Will this girls' night in make the boys switch off?

IN AMERICA, 'ALLY MCBEAL' HAS PROVED TO BE A HIT WITH ALL AUDIENCES, WRITES JANINE GIBSON. BUT BRITISH MEN MAY NOT WANT TO WATCH ANOTHER 'CHICK FLICK' SHOW

Ally McBeal, we are warned, 'Dares to Take you into the Mind of a Woman.'

The heroine, McBeal, is a lawyer who, after being sexually harassed, changes her job to join a firm in which her ex is employed. There is a five-person-strong ensemble cast, but stories are told from her perspective, with special effects inserts to show her thoughts as the plot moves along.

Its creator, David E Kelley, was asked by the Fox network to develop an hour-long series to run after Melrose Place and retain some of that audience. His brief was to write a series that would appeal to young women of 18–34 and provide an alternative to the predominantly male audience of *Monday Night Football* on the rival network ABC.

In an RTS speech earlier this year, Geoffrey Perkins, BBC head of comedy, said that six sitcoms currently airing in the US are about women in either publishing or PR. Certainly of those that has transferred to the UK, *Suddenly Susan* (Brooke Shields as a journalist), *Caroline in the City* (Lea Thompson as a syndicated cartoonist) and *Cybill* (Cybill Shepherd as an actress) bear out the 'media babe' obsession. All three women are around or above the age of 30; all are single; all face romantic tribulations in a comic way; and all are successful career women.

Source 4.13 (*The Independent*, 25 May 1998)

Advertising

It might be expected that advertising would make every effort to accurately reflect the changes in men's and women's lives in order to make their appeals more effective. This should particularly be the case for representations of women, as it is women who are responsible for the majority of purchasing decisions. It is true that adverts have changed over the years, as can be seen by comparing television adverts of the 1950s and 1960s with those of today. Previously, advertisers nearly always portrayed women in the home – washing, cleaning, looking after children and so on – while men were shown largely outside the home – at work or leisure.

Source 4.14a

Source 4.14 a, b and c

1 How far do these examples illustrate changes in the representations of males and females?
2 How typical are these of gender representation in modern advertising?

However, despite changes in the depiction of gender roles within advertising, there is criticism particularly from women, that advertising is still using outdated gender stereotypes. One explanation for the failure to adequately represent women could be the fact that most advertising agencies are dominated by men.

Source 4.14b

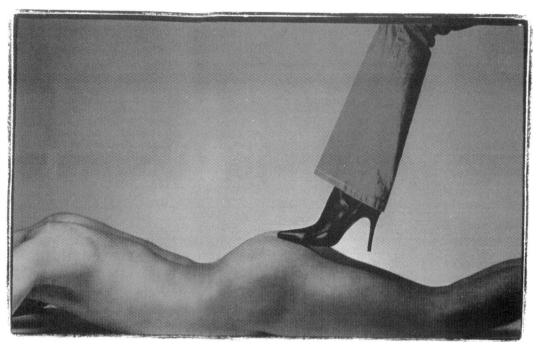

Put the boot in.

Bootcut jeans.

Source 4.14c

Gender and representation and production

Media production is still largely dominated by men. For example, in cinema there have only been a handful of female film producers or directors in the history of Hollywood and in Britain. With respect to newspapers, it was only in 1998 that Britain's first ever female editor of a national daily newspaper was appointed – Rosie Boycott at *The Express*. Within newspapers, female journalists tend to be concentrated in covering lifestyle features rather than political news or sports coverage.

The situation in television is rather better, with a more even number of male and female producers, but scriptwriters are overwhelmingly male. Furthermore, in 1999, only one of the main terrestrial television channels (Channel 5) had a female controller.

REPRESENTATIONS OF THE NATION

ACTIVITY

Make a list of things that you think illustrates what it means to be British – the Union Jack, for example.

It is likely that what it means to be British will vary according to individuals or groups of people. This may be affected by a range of social factors, such as country of origin, religion, sense of national pride and so on.

The media help to influence our sense of national identity in the way the nation is represented. This may be noticeable at times of national crisis or conflict, such as a war with another country – for example, during the Falklands War when the tabloid press helped to create a feeling of patriotism with references to 'our boys' fighting 'the Argies'. World War II films often have a similar effect, contributing towards pride in our history as a nation.

Sources 4.15 a and b

How do these two front pages help to construct a sense of national identity?

Source 4.15a

Source 4.15b

As a symbol of the nation, the Royal Family has been subject to a rich variety of media representations in recent years. Whereas television has continued to treat royalty with respect (for example, showing extended documentaries of both the Queen and Prince Charles fulfilling their duties), the national press has become much more critical, frequently revealing personal and embarrassing details of their private lives (such as the private telephone conversations exposing Prince Charles to be an adulterer).

This critical approach reached a peak following the death of Diana, Princess of Wales, in 1997. The Queen was seen as being too aloof from the national state of mourning and outpouring of grief (see Figure 4.2). Subsequently, the Royal Family has made great efforts to improve its image, particularly in its dealings with the media, but it is unlikely that it can restore its position as a symbol of a united nation.

Source 4.16b (*Today*, 10 June 1994)

Sources 4.16 a and b

Contrast these two representations of the Royal family.

Choosing presents for the family that has everything

continued from page 29 from the room. The Queen likes to make this strictly a family affair.

The reason for exchanging gifts on Christmas Eve dates back to Queen Alexandra's time. Edward VII's wife was born in Denmark, where people open their presents the night before Christmas.

After this opening ceremony, most of the treasures are left on display on the table, but the children race off around the castle, trying out new toys or showing them off to everyone.

The Queen likes to give books – non-fiction, thrillers or biographies to Prince Charles and her husband. The Duke of York gets the latest technical books on photography and, in exchange, he often gives his mother a framed photograph he has taken himself.

Close friends often receive yet another book

on breeding dogs or bloodstock from the Queen. She is not so keen on burying her nose in a book herself, so relatives usually give her dog leads, headscarves, or photograph albums.

One Christmas, she received a pair of porcelain candlesticks as her main gift from the Prince and Princess of Wales. But, when the Prince filled a stocking for his mother – the way he

Presents for outdoor types suit the Duke of York and Duke of Edinburgh (above). The Queen Mother (right) receives gifts of little luxuries from her loved ones.

has done ever since he was a teenager – the Princess popped in some corgi-shaped soaps she had bought from Crabtree & Evelyn in Kensington. Princess Anne likes practical gifts and once

asked a member of her staff to make sure that Prince Charles gave her the doormat she needed for her home at Gatcombe Park. In return, she knows he always loves receiving any kind of fishing tackle. The Queen Mother is

known to love little luxuries, so the Princess of Wales gave her a pale-blue swansdown powder-puff two years ago.

Prince Edward's interest in the theatre guarantees that he will get new books continued on page 33

Source 4.16a (*TV Times*, 19 December 1987)

National identity may also be strengthened during international sporting contests, such as the Olympic Games or the World Cup. On such occasions, British competitors or teams are referred to as 'us' as opposed to 'them', the opposition. This leads us on to consider how people from other nations might be represented in the media.

Figure 4.2 (*The Guardian*, 5 September 1997)

REPRESENTATIONS OF RACE/ETHNICITY

There are many stereotypes of people on the basis of their ethnic group – that is, their shared national culture.

Media representations of ethnic groups, and people from other countries in general, vary from the exotic and interesting, to the strange and threatening. Where ideas support the view that our culture is superior to others, then this is called **ethnocentrism**. Where ideas support the belief that other people are inferior, then this is called **racism**. Racism has tended to draw on physical differences between people, especially skin colour. Such beliefs can be traced back to colonial rule in the case of Britain. It is easier to dominate and exploit people when it is thought (falsely) that they are less developed or more primitive.

Source 4.17 a

Which ethnic stereotype is represented in this programme?

ACTIVITY

Make a list of stereotypes for the following groups:

- Irish
- Welsh
- Scots
- English
- Italians
- French
- Germans
- Australians
- Americans
- Japanese
- Iranians

1 For which of the above groups have you found it easiest and hardest to think of stereotypes?
2 Why is it so easy or difficult to think of stereotypes for these groups?

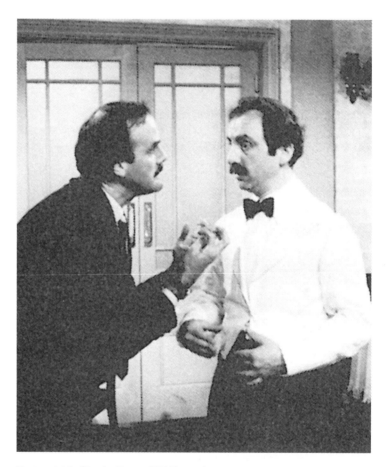

Source 4.17 (*Fawlty Towers*, BBC Enterprises Limited 1979)

Figure 4.3 (P. Oliver, *The Story of the Blues*, Penguin, 1972)

NOTICE!
STOP

HELP SAVE THE YOUTH OF AMERICA

DON'T BUY NEGRO RECORDS

(If you don't want to serve negroes in your place of business, then do not have negro records on your juke box or listen to negro records on the radio.)

The screaming, idiotic words, and savage music of these records are undermining the morals of our white youth in America. Call the advertisers of the radio

---

The 'screaming, idiotic words, and savage music' – then called rhythm and blues – later became known as rock and roll, and is still the basis for today's rock/pop music enjoyed by people throughout the Western world.

A similar kind of fear and hatred has been voiced about more modern black American music, in particular rap. The aggressive and defiant attitude represented in much of the lyrics and video performances of rap artists (especially 'gangsta rap') has led to attempts to censor or ban some of the music.

Source 4.18

How might this image of rappers be interpreted?

Source 4.18

Sources 4.19 a and b

How do these two images differ in their representation of black people?

It would seem that compared to older Hollywood images of black people as simple and fun-loving as in *Gone With The Wind*, modern images are more

Source 4.19a (*TV Times*, 21 November 1987)

Source 4.19b (Bob Hope and Willie Best in *The Ghost Breakers*)

likely to be positive. In the cinema, actors such as Denzel Washington and Will Smith star in leading roles, and on television Lenny Henry and Bill Cosby have had their own successful comedy shows. However, despite some improvement in the situation, there is still an absence of black people and those from other ethnic minorities in much of the media output.

ACTIVITIES

1. Select one television genre – soap opera, sitcom, police series or whatever – and examine which and how ethnic minorities are represented within that genre during a week's television output. Identify the number of ethnic minority characters represented and the narrative context in which they appear. Do they have leading or secondary roles? Do they fit closely typical stereotypes of such groups? Do any particular patterns emerge?

2. Record 30 television adverts and identify the number and range of ethnic minorities represented within the adverts. How representative are the adverts of a multicultural Britain? Are there any particular products advertised in which ethnic minorities are likely to feature.

Race and the news

Sources 4.20 a and b

1 What do these images and headlines say about black people in Britain?
2 Would the label 'white' be applied to the stories if white people had been involved?
3 How might the *Daily Mail* story be told by a black reporter who had close ties with the Handsworth community? Think about how such labels as 'riot', 'mob' and 'hooligan' might be changed in this case.

Few journalists set out to stir up racial hatred. Part of the explanation for such reporting is that it is based on news values of drama, threat, spectacle and so on (as discussed on pages 52–4) in an attempt to boost circulation or ratings. Little space exists for background explanation, such as the long-term effects of poverty, conflict with the police and racial harassment. Furthermore, most journalists are white and reflect the views of the dominant cultural group in society. The views of minority groups are rarely voiced because very few are employed within the media (see Figure 4.4).

As a result, many ethnic minority people distrust the mainstream media as a source of news and instead turn to other sources, especially news media produced by and for such communities (see Figure 4.5).

Ethnic minority journalists on London-based national papers

Daily Mail	**Independent**	**Observer**
Editors: 0	Editors: 1	Editors: 0
Writers/reporters: 2	Writers/reporters: 3	Writers/reporters: 2
Daily Telegraph	Columnists: 1	**Sunday Mirror**
Editors: 0	**Mirror**	Editors: 0
Writers/reporters: 1	Editors: 0	Writers/reporters: 0
The Express/	Writers/reporters: 2	**Sunday People**
Sunday Express	**Sun:**	Editors: 0
Editors: 3	Editors: 0	Writers/reporters: 2
Writers/reporters: 3	Writers/reporters: 1	**Sunday Telegraph**
Columnists:	**Times**	Editors: 0
Financial	Editors: 0	Writers/reporters: 1
Times	Writers/reporters: 1	**Sunday Times**
Editors: 0	**Mail on Sunday**	Editors: 1
Writers/reporters: 6	Editors: 0	Writers/reporters: 3
Guardian	Writers/reporters: 0	*Information from press or personnel offices, or managing editors. Significantly, many said they did not keep such information so some data is unconfirmed. Research by Muriel Desailles*
Editors: 5	**News of the World**	
Writers/reporters: 3	Editors: 0	
	Writers/reporters: 1	

Baz Bamigboye of the Daily Mail

Figure 4.4 (*The Guardian*, 1 March 1999)

Figure 4.5 (*The Voice*, 22 November 1999)

Source 4.20a (*Daily Mail*, 11 September 1985)

Source 4.20b

Multicultural representation

This means reflecting the fact that Britain is made up of more than one culture — that is, ways of life, religions, customs and beliefs. How far the mainstream British media accurately reflects the multicultural society in which we live is open to question.

It is easier to find cultural diversity represented in what could be called 'minority' media production. Within television, this includes BBC2 and Channel 4, which have broadcast a wide range of programmes, often produced by teams of people from different ethnic backgrounds. Two successful comedy series from BBC2 are *The Real McCoy* and *Goodness Gracious Me* (originally broadcast on radio). These are unusual in that they provide a different (racial/ethnic) comedy perspective from that which dominates on BBC1 and ITV.

Figure 4.6 (*Goodness Gracious Me*)

The rise of cable television and expansion of local radio services has enabled ethnic groups to receive their own culturally specific programmes (see Figure 4.7).

Figure 4.7

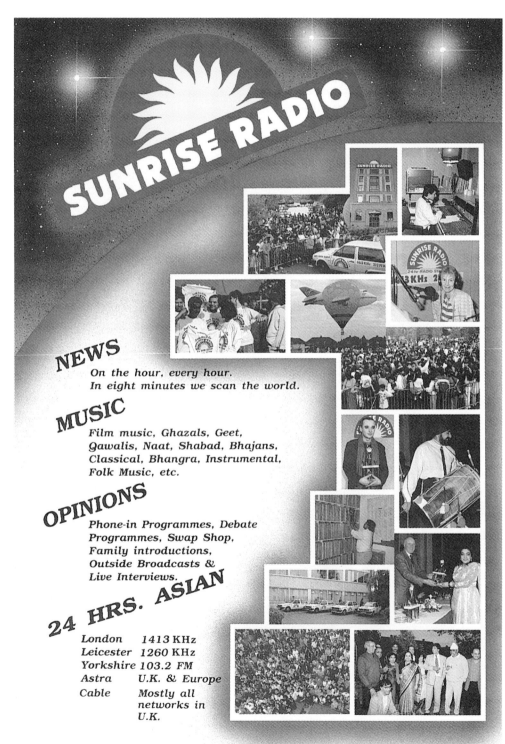

NEWS

On the hour, every hour.
In eight minutes we scan the world.

MUSIC

Film music, Ghazals, Geet, Qawalis, Naat, Shabad, Bhajans, Classical, Bhangra, Instrumental, Folk Music, etc.

OPINIONS

Phone-in Programmes, Debate Programmes, Swap Shop, Family introductions, Outside Broadcasts & Live Interviews.

24 HRS. ASIAN

London	1413 KHz
Leicester	1260 KHz
Yorkshire	103.2 FM
Astra	U.K. & Europe
Cable	Mostly all networks in U.K.

ONE TELEPHONE CALL - YOUR DIRECT LINE TO MILLION ASIANS.

Images of the Third World

The further away a foreign culture or country is, the less likely it is to feature within the British media. This is particularly true of Third World countries – a label used for poorer, less industrialized countries in Africa, Asia and Latin America. It usually requires something very dramatic to happen – such as a war or natural disaster – before such countries are mentioned in news or current affairs coverage.

Sources 4.21 a, b and c

1 How do each of these images represent Africa?
2 Why do they seem inconsistent?
3 Where are you likely to find such images in the media?
4 How might they affect ideas and attitudes towards black people in Britain?

Source 4.21a

Source 4.21b

Source 4.21c

Childhood

Until this century, most children did not have a special status in society. In fact, they were seen as miniature adults, who would usually work and contribute to the family as soon as physically possible. We now see children very differently.

There is a tendency to idealize and romanticize childhood – as a period of innocence and freedom but also of vulnerability. This is particularly noticeable in Hollywood where child stars are usually cute and lovable, and triumph over the odds, especially evil adults (such as in the *Home Alone* films). Alternatively, children may be seen as victims, in horror films such as *The Exorcist* or news reports of child abuse and violence.

The most notable challenge to these stereotypical representations of children can be found in the new wave of American cartoons that have arisen following the success of *The Simpsons*. Bart Simpson is a widely recognized symbol of childhood rebellion. He does everything adults seek to prevent children from doing, and yet remains a likeable and funny character. Later cartoons, and especially *South Park*, have further explored the less attractive and 'darker' side of children's nature.

Source 4.22a

Source 4.22b

Youth

For as long as there has been popular culture and the mass media, there has been adult concern about young people, especially teenagers. Much of the concern has revolved around young people's use of the media and the potential harmful effects (see pages 32–3). This concern has been voiced by and through the media in Britain, notably the popular press. They have singled out groups of young people as social problems. **Folk devils** is a term that has been used to refer to images of people we should reject. Youths are often labelled as folk devils, in need of social control.

Source 4.23

1 Who are the folk devils here?
2 Why do you think young people are labelled as folk devils by the press? (See pages 52–4 on news values.)
3 Are there any young folk devils currently appearing in the press?

Moral panics

Often, within the media, a group of people or type of behaviour come to be seen as a threat to society. This is called a **moral panic**. A campaign develops, usually involving politicians and people in authority, who draw attention to what they think is a problem. Moral panics in the past have been about football hooligans, drug addicts, muggers, glue-sniffers, student rebels, pot-smokers and, more recently, raves and ecstasy. Each problem is simplified, those blamed are given a bad name, public opinion is whipped up against them, and all this leads to stronger controls by those in authority.

ACTIVITY

See if you can spot a moral panic in the popular press. Try to answer the following questions.

1 What is the problem?
2 Which person or group is identified as the cause?
3 How is it labelled?
4 Whose views of people in positions of authority are given (MPs, police, experts and so on)?
5 What suggestions are made for controlling and solving the problem?

Source 4.23 (*Daily Mirror*, 18 May 1964)

After Clacton.. a new battlefield

Daily Mirror

WILD ONES 'BEAT UP' MARGATE

40 arrested in all-day clashes

THE GIRLS FIGHT IT OUT

BLACK EYE

Marketing youth

What may originally be a threatening or shocking image can, over time, become tamed or defused by the media and made into something more safe (and profitable). For example, it was not long before 'punk'-style characters began to appear in adverts for such things as opening a bank account. James Dean is often thought of as one of the first youth rebels. (He died in a car crash in 1955.)

Source 4.24a

Sources 4.24 a and b

How are these representations of 'rebellious' youth being used?

Given that the key audience for cinema going is 15–24-year-olds, it is not surprising that many films have teenage culture as their subject. Since the 1950s, the themes of the pains of growing up, being accepted, finding an identity and so on have been extensively examined. These films often have quite an optimistic and upbeat message that problems of sexual identity, parental conflict and so on can be resolved. However, a number of recent films have also explored the bleaker and more pessimistic experiences of young people's lives, such as *Trainspotting* and *Kids*.

Source 4.24b

Krizia uomo. Break the rules.

Krizia uomo. After Shave, Eau de Toilette, After Shave Balm, Savon de Toilette, Deodorant.

ACTIVITY

1 Compare two films that feature teenage/high school culture.
2 What are the main themes with respect to dramatic conflict (such as teenagers versus adult authority, conformity versus non-conformity)? How are differences in gender, ethnicity or class represented?
3 To what extent is being young idealized or romanticized?

Old age

Research into media representations of old age in America and Britain has shown that the elderly (60 and over) are generally viewed rather negatively. A common image is that of the old person as a victim – of violence, deprivation, loneliness, ill health and so on. Discriminating against people on the grounds of their age is referred to as **ageism**.

ACTIVITIES

1 From the press, collect four stories that feature the elderly.
   How are they represented in each story?
   Why have they been chosen as news stories?
   How are they physically described?

2 Choose four elderly characters from television soap operas and sitcoms. To what extent are they represented as:
   • wise/foolish
   • comfortable/badly off
   • fit/unfit
   • sexually active/inactive
   • tolerant/intolerant
   • powerful/powerless
   • independent/dependent
   • respected/not respected?

Age	TV (%)	Real World (%)
1–24	12	30
25–34	32	16
35–44	29	14
45–59	20	18
60 and over	7	21
Total	**100**	**99**

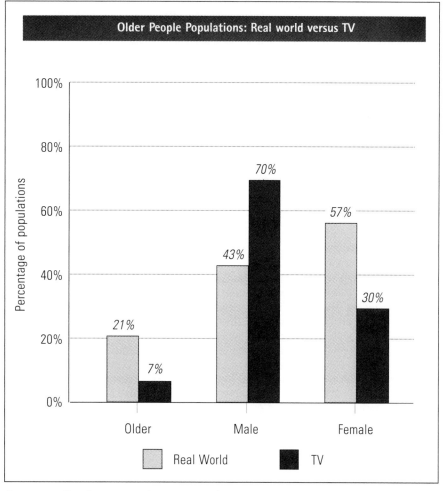

Source 4.25 (Age Concern, *Too Old for TV?*, 1999)

Estelle reaches her golden age

When The Golden girls get together each Friday on C4, it's hardly Listen with Mother time. They may look like a twittery sewing circle made up of everyone's favourite aunts, mothers and grandmas, but their needles could be sharpened on their tongues.

Topics you'd think would make your granny's perm frizzle are discussed with unflinching regularity: sex (too much and too little) more sex, the pros and cons of dating midgets, drooping breasts, plastic surgery, heart attacks, death, drugs, incontinence, wind, abortion, ex-husbands, hot flushes and funerals.

"It's honest," says Betty White, who plays sweet, vague, rambling Rose "The show's about real life. Probably if young actresses discussed taboo subjects the way we do, the show would be bleeped. They'd be accused of doing it for shock value. But we four ladies have been round the Horn several times. We're having so much fun, it should be illegal. It's nice to know you don't self-destruct after 40".

The four ladies – Betty, Bea Arthur (Dorothy), Rue McClanahan (Blanche) and Estelle Getty (Sophia) – think the show is in Rue's words, "a gift from the gods". It rescued them from endless bit-parts and Love Boat guest-starring roles, has given them sizeable nest-eggs, changed the life of New York-based stage actress Estelle and made them all symbols of success for the over-60s (something that Rue, 52 and a good 10 years younger than her co-stars, bristles at – much like her character Blanche, the desperate divorcee who will be 30 till the day she dies).

Source 4.26 (*TV Times*, 7 November 1987)

Source 5.1a

Source 5.1b

GENRE CATEGORIES

Sources 5.1 a, b and c

These three pictures are taken from films.

1 What kinds of films are they?
2 What sorts of themes and plots are likely to occur?
3 Which characters would you expect to appear?
4 Where is the action likely to take place?
5 What are typical titles of such films?

When similar types of films, television programmes, music and so on are grouped together, they are referred to as a **genre**. They are thought to have common codes and conventions. In particular, they are likely to share some or all of the following:

- **Narrative** – storylines, themes, resolutions (how the stories are brought to a conclusion);
- **Characters** – leading and secondary roles (heroes, villains and so on), their appearance and behaviour;
- **Settings** – time and place;
- **Audio-visual codes** – the camera work, lighting, sound, editing and so on (as discussed in Chapter 2).

Source 5.1c

Depending on which media form is involved, the particular elements that contribute to a genre will vary. For example, with film genres, there is usually a strong emphasis on the **visual look** which may give the film a distinctive genre identity.

Consider the example of the **Western** film (see Figure 5.1). It is traditionally recognized by the following:

- **Narrative** themes of revenge, law and order, civilizing the West;
- **Characters**
  - *roles* sheriff, gunfighters, pioneers, cavalry, Indians, outlaws, gamblers and so on;
  - *appearance* certain clothes (hats, boots, holsters and so on) – the heroes in white and clean-shaven, the villains in black and unshaven;
- **Settings** outdoors, plains, deserts, mountains, frontier towns, ranches, forts; mostly mid to late nineteenth-century North America;
- **Audio-visual codes** use of extreme long shots, western music (harmonica, twanging guitar and so on).

In addition, audiences may recognize Westerns from their titles (*Gunfight at the OK Corral*, *My Darling Clementine*) stars (John Wayne, Gary Cooper) and theme music (*The Good the Bad and the Ugly*, *The Magnificent Seven*).

ACTIVITY

Select one of the following film genres:
- musical,
- gangster,
- science fiction
- horror.

Identify how each of the headings listed on page 97 applies to that genre.

Problems with genre categories

If you compare your list to those made by others, you will find you have noted different aspects. Genres can never be precisely defined categories. As cultural products, films and other media texts need to be individually distinctive for audiences to enjoy them – unlike industrial products, which are usually made in a standardized form.

Each new media text may help to develop the genre – no genre is static, it is always evolving. New examples may develop the range of themes and characters. For example, in the 1960s Westerns (so called 'spaghetti Westerns' because they were directed by Italian Sergio Leone) were very different from the John Wayne Westerns of the 1940s and 1950s. The 'hero' of such films (usually Clint Eastwood – see Figure 5.2) was no longer clearly in the right, and the violence became much more bloody. When a new pattern, such as the 'spaghetti Western', emerges that is distinctively different from the traditional genre, then this is called a **subgenre**.

A further complication is that some media texts may contain elements of two or more genres. In the case of the Western, there have been musical Westerns (*Paint Your Wagon*), science fiction Westerns (*Westworld*) and comedy Westerns (*Cat Ballou*). Within television, an example of a **crossover genre** is the docusoap, discussed in Chapter 2.

Finally, it is worth remembering that some media texts defy genre categories. Because they are so individual or original, they have little in common with other texts. However, this is unusual because of commercial factors.

Production and audience

In Chapter 3, it was noted that one of the key factors influencing media production was the need for profit. Labelling a film 'horror' or 'science fiction' helps audiences decide whether or not they might enjoy seeing the film. In other words, audience recognition is a key marketing principle.

Film studios used to specialize in particular genres – for example, MGM in musicals and Warner Brothers in gangster films. It helped to minimize costs by employing production teams and facilities that could almost operate as a conveyor belt for similar genre-based films. However, as the uncertainty of cinema audience tastes has grown (see William Goldman's comments on page 44), more emphasis is placed on repeating the formula for individually successful films. This has led to 'mini' genres in the form of sequel cycles such as the *Star Wars* and *Police Academy* films.

Figure 5.1

Sources 5.2 a and b

To which genres do these films belong?

Source 5.2b

Source 5.2a

Figure 5.2

TELEVISION GENRES

Soap opera

Soap operas originated in America. The name comes from the fact that the programmes were sponsored by manufacturers of soap powder. Traditional American soap is broadcast daily during the day, unlike in Britain.

Source 5.3

1 How are the plots similar to, and different from, British soaps?
2 *Neighbours* is an example of an Australian soap opera that is broadcast on weekdays by the BBC. What differences, in terms of plot, themes and characters, are there between *Neighbours* and *Brookside*, which is also set in a suburban close?

Source 5.3 (*Cleveland Plain Dealer*, 1 April 1984)

Here are summaries of last week's soap opera plots

Loving

Isabel confused when Cabot is upset at thought of inviting Shana to dinner.

Jim admits to Shana he still has feelings for her but his priestly vows come first. Warren warns Mike he has to see the psychiatrist or he'll be dropped from the police force. Lorna, offered job as a model, decides to have abortion without telling Tony. Rose unhappy about Stacey dating Curtis. Loran talks her parents into letting Tony and her live at gatehouse and later tells Tony it was her grandparents' idea. Rita Mae finally realizes how much Billy wants a child and agrees to start a family. Suffering writer's block, Doug is going to New York to talk to producer of new play and hopes to regain his writing ability.

One life to live

Going against advice of lawyers, Vicki decides to let workers take over plant. When bankers will not give money to workers, Bo/Bill secretly guarantees loan. Tired of living at boarding house, Bo asks to move into O'Neill household. Harry agrees and gives him room belonging to Didi, the oldest O'Neill daughter who is away at college. The night Bo/Bill moves into the room, Didi, who has decided to quit school, shows up. Jenny, having decided to break up with David, heads for retreat. Brad appears and she learns that he arranged for Liat to stop wedding ceremony. Feeling totally shattered by Brad's confession, Jenny decides to return to nunnery. Herb, realizing he still loves Dorian, asks her to come home when she is released from hospital and he will help with paralysis treatment. Herb asked to head commission to halt suburban mob influence. Dee fired by Anthony.

Ryan's hope

A drunken Roger makes a phone call to Maggie, who panics. Frank rushes to her side. They share a passionate kiss and Bess is stunned when she discovers Maggie and Frank in Maggie's bed. Bess blames Maggie, but apologizes when she realizes Roger tried to rape Maggie. Roger tells Frank he remembers nothing of the phone call. Fearing he's having alcoholic blackouts, Roger decides to stop drinking, but soon breaks his promise. In Nice, Seneca suggests Jill was happier when she was married to him. Jill angry when Seneca says if Roger keeps drinking, his job is over at the hospital. Johnny becomes furious when he walks in and spots a leotard-clad Katie in the living room with Rick. Pat tells Johnny that Katie's old enough to have boyfriends visit her. Maggie goes on commercial interview and is assured job if she'll sleep with the director. Katie and Maggie talk Dave into turning loft into living quarters for them.

Search for tomorrow

Feeling he's caused Suzi to leave town, Cagney starts drinking. Warren tells Wendy that Cagney is father of Suzi's child. Sunny insists on return to work but becomes hysterical when she realizes that Jack, who was acquitted of rape charges, is also working at the station. Cagney pays visit to comatose Justine in the hospital and is stunned when he runs into Suzi, who has applied for a job there. Warren horrified to learn share in nightclub he won from Martin is useless as Martin recently sold his interest to Lloyd.

Young and the restless

Carole tells Jack she wants him to look at her as a woman, not just a friend. Jack fears Carl is aware of the problem he and Jill are having. Lindsay informs Jack his turning his back on her made her become black-mailer. When Diane is offered New York modelling job, Andy offers to leave town with her. Liz is worried about Kaye's surgery, while Jill hopes she dies during the face lift. Dina relieved when she thinks Mark is leaving town. Mark gets letter from his sister Danielle, who reminds him they must have revenge on Dina. Tracy upset because she was unable to make love to Tim.

© *News America Syndicate*

Within soap opera, much of the action takes place in a distinctive area – a street, village or house. There is usually a limited number of characters, whose relationships form the basis for the plot. Part of the pleasure for viewers (or listeners for radio soap opera) is the constant posing of questions – what will happen next? Audiences are frequently left to ponder on how characters will react to a dilemma, or what may happen to them in the next episode. Because each episode ends with stories left unfinished, the last scene is referred to as a **cliffhanger**. This can vary from high drama to comic surprise.

Many viewers often react to the lives of soap actors as if they were real people, sending them get well cards, wedding cards and so on. The programme makers seem to go to great lengths to make the end product appear real. For example, in *Brookside*, Mersey Television actually bought real houses for the setting.

EastEnders
Tuesday and Thursday
7.00 BBC1

Ask any EastEnder for directions to Albert Square, London Borough of Walford, E20, and they'll tell you "Straight down Turpin Road Market, turn right into Bridge Street, and there it is with the Queen Vic pub on the corner."

Ask anyone and they'll tell you that the two best-known families in the square are the Beales and the Fowlers. "Lived here since the year dot!" **Lou Beale**, in her 70s is head of a large cockney family. She's plump, loud, funny and sentimental – but can be stubborn, too.

Two of Lou's children have stayed in the East End: Pauline and Pete – **Pauline Fowler**, who does the morning shift at the local launderette, is married to Arthur and they have two teenage kids, **Mark** and **Michelle**. They share Lou's house: 45 Albert Square.

Pauline's twin brother, **Pete**, who has a fruit 'n' veg stall in Bridge Street, lives with his second wife, **Kathy** and son **Ian** in a flat on the nearby 'estate'.

Ask anyone about the Beales and the Fowlers. **Den Watts,** for instance, the guv'nor of the Queen Vic, is Pete Beale's best mate. Pete's barrow is right outside the pub. Since the lads were school kids Den's always been on the fiddle, and Pete's always covered for him. S'what mates are for, innit?

Ask anyone who holds that pub together, and they'll say "She does! **Angie** is no fool" Lately, the publican's wife is starting to wonder if she's the one who's being 'fiddled' by Jack-the-lad Den. Tricky that, seeing as Angie's best mate is Kathy, Pete's wife, and Kathy doesn't lie. It's all a bit

tough on Den and Angie's adopted daughter, **Sharon** – piggy-in-the-middle.

There are not many people in Albert Square **Dr Harold Legg** doesn't know – he brought them into the world. Lou Beale can't work out why he keeps his surgery in the square, as he moved home out of the district years ago. An old-fashioned 'family doctor', he goes back a long way with Lou. He can see right through her and knows when she's being the battleaxe, that it's all an act so that she can get her own way – which is most of the time!

Dr Legg's cleaning lady, **Ethel Skinner,** lives in the flat above the surgery. She's Lou Beale's greatest friend. You can't miss Ethel: she's always wearing a hat and always followed by her little dog, Willy. She also cleans the pub – when she turns up, that is! She's inclined to get carried away telling fortunes in the market or getting conned into doing laundry for Lofty.

Lofty Holloway occupies the flat above Ethel. Funny lad, Lofty. He's got the gift of the gab all right, can charm the birds off the trees. But keeps vanishing – for days on end. Lofty does work now and then. Like three sessions behind the bar at the pub – cash in hand, of course.

Ali and **Sue Osman** and nine-month-old baby **Hassan**, live in a council flat in the run-down side of Albert Square. They run Ali's Cafe in Bridge Street, just across the road from the Vic and frequented by the market traders. Ali, a Turkish Cypriot, is likeable but lazy, and gambles away half the cafe's takings, which doesn't keep Sue in the best of moods. She's sharp-tongued at the best of times. And that's what gets up Kathy Beale's nose.

In the room above Sue and Ali's (and sharing the bathroom) is **Mary Smith** and her nine-week-old daughter **Annie.** No one in the square is convinced she is going to be able to manage. Lou says that

Mary's a bit young to be bringing up a child alone. Sue Osman reckons she clutters up the bathroom.

Ask anyone if there's a builder, decorator, handyman in the square and they'll point you in the direction of number 3, where **Tony Carpenter** lives. Or will live when he finishes 'doing it up'. Meanwhile, he sleeps in his van. Tony is about to get a divorce, and his wife is convinced he won't stay in Walford. Tony has no staying power, she believes.

Kelvin, Tony's son, is studying for his GCSEs. He could do without the aggro between his parents. He's also got problems with Michelle Fowler and Sharon Watts, the rivals for his affections.

Opposite Al's Cafe is the Foodstore run by two young Bengalis, **Saeed** and **Naima Jeffery,** who live round the corner in the square. Their marriage was hastily arranged because Saeed's parents had to return to India and wanted someone to keep the business going. But shop work is very new and confusing for them – rather similar to their relationship. If you ask Lou Beale, she will tell you the shop carries 'too much foreign muck'.

And there are newcomers in the square, too. **Debs** and **Andy** are working-class professionals (she works in a bank, he's a children's nurse). But to most of the inhabitants of Albert Square they're 'outsiders' – posh, even. Lou says Debs is too bossy by half – really 'stuck up'. Andy makes excuses for her.

Families and family life play a large part in everyday happenings in Albert Square. Who's doing what, to whom and where is the constant chat of the neighbourhood. Gossip, intrigue and scandal are high on the list of daily events. Ask anyone ....

TONY HOLLAND

Source 5.4 (*Radio Times*, 16 February 1985)

Newspaper format

National daily and Sunday newspapers are often divided between 'quality' broadsheet and 'popular' tabloid. One obvious difference between them is the size. Broadsheets are twice the size of tabloid newspapers. This is one of the aspects of a newspaper's **format** – which is the size, shape, and content of the publication.

There are differences within broadsheet and tabloid formats. Some tabloids, such as the *Daily Mail* and *The Express*, occupy a midway position between broadsheets, such as *The Times* and *The Independent*, and the 'pop' tabloids – *The Sun, The Mirror* and *Daily Star*.

Figure 5.4

Compare the format of a national broadsheet newspaper to that of a popular tabloid. (You could start with the examples shown on pages 17–18.) Comment on the following aspects:

1 *design*
   - size of print and photographs;
   - number of stories per page;
   - layout of stories and photographs;
   - general graphics, such as print (use of italics or bold print), boxes, underlining captions, quotes and so on.
2 *content*
   how many pages and column inches are devoted to:
   - news – how much is British or foreign news, which stories are covered, are there news features;
   - entertainment and arts coverage;
   - other features, such as finance and business, sport (which sports), letters, astrology, crossword competitions?

Magazines

Magazine formats vary much more than those of newspapers. Women's magazines are the biggest sector (see page 114 for a list of the top 100 magazines). The major high street newsagents subdivide the main categories or genres, so that buyers can easily find most titles in their respective categories.

Select two examples of magazines or comics aimed at either children or teenagers. Examine the form of each with respect to:
1 design – print, photographs, layout and so on.
2 categories of content.

These samples of single and album releases in one week contain over 20 categories of music. As with all genres, individual categories overlap – for example dance and techno or country and folk. It is doubtful that audiences apply the same labels that are used in the industry. What then makes a music genre?

Source 5.5

How do album releases differ from single releases in terms of the music genres represented?

Sound

The most obvious ingredient is the sound – the choice of instruments, the singing style and possibly the lyrics.

Style

Apart from the visual style, there is the style of the performers and the audience. These include clothes, hair, accessories – the overall *look* associated with the music.

Meaning

The meanings created by differing musical sounds and styles depend on the surrounding culture. Pop music has always been linked to youth culture. Much of the pleasure of rock and roll in the 1950s was that it expressed a sense of rebellion and sexual excitement that appealed to teenagers (and upset adults, who sometimes tried to ban it).

Source 5.5 (*Music Week*, 19 July 1999)

Singles

12 Tree	Woodland Funk	Dance/Leftfield
3 Jays, The	Feeling It too	Dance
3's Company	Come and Tell Me	Dance
702	Where my Girl's At	Dance/R&B
Adapt-Synth	Take Off	Dance
Alice Dee Jay	Better Off Alone	Dance
Arturo	Former	Pop/rock
Atmos	The Only Process	Dance
Baker, Arthur & Rennie Pilgrim	Hey Funky People	Breakbeat
Bang	Into the Millennium	Happycore
Basement Jaxx	Rendez Vous	House
Basic	Greenback	Dance
Boredom UK	Seditionaries Revisited	Indie
Brian	Turn your Lights On	Pop/Indi
BSO Research	Gap Tools	Breakbeat
Bushwacka	Grief	Breakbeat
Cadillacs	Johnny Remember Me	Pop
Casa Nostra	Our House	Dance
Choc! Strange	When you're Twisted	Trance/Acid
Chop Suey	The BoyGirl	Big Beat
Christian West	Eterna	Dance
Circle 99	I Want it that Way	Pop/Dance
Clan Grego	Rotation	House
Click	Sonic Eclipse	Dance
Clock	Sunshine Day	Pop
Console	Pan or Ama	Electronica
Contempo	UB Naughty	Pop/rock
Costello, Elvis	She	Pop/MOR/Films
Cox, Deborah	It's Over	Pop/Dance/R&B
Criptic	Fly Day	Indie
Darshan	Freaky Frequency	Trance
Decoder/Substance	Heist	Drum & Bass
Disco Enforcers	Jumpin	House/Disco
Discotexx	Hot Cops	House
DJDab	Surround	Dance/Leftfield
DJ Producer	The Runner	Techno/Hardcore
DJ Skippy	Till I Come	Happycore
DJ Slip	Stone Broke	Dance
DJ Storm	Rave	Happycore
Dr Doom	Leave Me Alone	Hip Hop
Dub Duo	I Love You	Dance
Dylan & Fags	Plankton	Drum & Bass
Emulator	No Fate	Dance
Entity Squad	Could Be So	House
Erot	Two Songs for Annie	Dance
Esion God	Trials and Tripulations	Trance
Ethnica	The Plar	Trance
Family of God	Generica America	Indie
Fields, Jordan	Off the Mutha Funkin Hook	House
Five	If You're Gettin Down	Pop
Flying Grooves	Roll & Co	House
For You	4 U	Techno
Fridge	Of	Electronic/ Post Rock
Frost, Edith	Love is Real	Indie
G.D. Luxxe	Superamerica	Electro
Gentleman Thief	We Generate Love	Dance/Leftfield
Germinator	Zumo	Trance
Glory's	When I see Your Body	House
Gray, David	Babylon	Indie
Hamma, Ibrahim	Dicko	Dance
High Fidelity Present	Cream of Beats	Jazz/breakbeat
Horne, Espen	Magnetica	
Hot Toddy	2000	House/Disco
Iglesias, Julio, JR	One More Chance	Pop/Latin
Jadell	Compared to What	Dance/Downbeat

Al Jabr	One Million and Three	Electronica
Andromeda	See Into the Stars	Progressive
Anti Flag	A New Kind of Army	Punk
Appendix Out	Daylight Saving	Indie
At Jazz	That Something	House
Atkins, Chet, & Jerry Reed	Me & Jerry/Me & Chet	Country/Rock
Atlantic Starr	Legacy	Soul
Ausgang	Electric Arc	Rock/Leftfield
Average White Band	Face to Face Live	Pop/Soul
Basskraft	A Bass Tribute to Craftwerk	Electro
Brown, Charles	In a Grand Style	Jazz/R&B
Butthole Surfers	Rembrandt Pussyhorse	Indie
Campbell Al	Roots & Culture	Reggae
Caustic Resin	The Medicine is All Gone	Indie
Ceol Band & Singers, The	Celtic Spirit	Rock/Celtic
Cogs, The	Viva	Indie
Copeland, Johnny	Honky Tonkin	Blues/R&B
Crown of Thorns	Breakthrough	Rock
Dashboard Dandies, The	Sonic Surprises	Pop
Savis, Skeeter	Skeeter Davis Sings Buddy Holly/Skeeter Sings Doll	Pop
Death Ride 69	Screaming Down the Gravity Well	Industrial
Delta 72	Sorega Doushita	Indie
Deviants, The/Mick Farren	3/Mona The Carnivorous Circus	Rock
Different Levels	The Next Step	Drum & Bass
DJ Chrome	Hypnotic Drum N Bass	Drum & Bass/Relaxation
Down by Law	Fly the Flag	Punk
Doyle, Mike	Every Word	MOR
Drugstore Cowboys, The	Crash & Burn	Rockabilly
Earthtone 9	Offkilter Enhancement	Metal/Hardcore
El Stew	El Stew	Dance/Leftfield
**Ensign	Cast the First Stone	Punk/Hardcore
**EPMD	Out of Business/Greatest Hits	Hip Hop
Exploding Thumbs, The	Beginning of Blue	Dance/Leftfield
Fighting Cocks, The	Come and See	Indie
Flinch	All Day Breakfast	Pop
Freeway	Bruised	Indie
Get Animal	Get Animal	Rock
Gibson, Don	Girls, Guitars & Gibson/Too Much Hurt	Country
Gilberto, Astrus	The Girl from Panema	Pop/MOR
Gillan	Japanese Album	Rock
GNAC	Friend Sleeping	Indie
Gondwana	Together	Reggae
Gong	The Best of Gong	Prog Rock
Gramme	Pre-Release	Indie/Leftfield
Heptones, The	They Came, They Saw, They	Reggae
Hersch, Fred, Trio	Plays Coleman Coltrane Davis Etc	Jazz
Hidenobu ITO	Bedroom in the Cage	Electronica
Hirota, Joji	The Gate	World
Honeysuckle Rose	A Tribute to the Marvellous Music of Fats Waller	Rock n' Roll
Iron Monkey/Church of Misery	Split Album	Metal
Jones, Patrick	Commemoration and Amnesia	Indie
James Ingram	Forever More	Soul
Katmandu	A Case for the Blues	Blues
Kleczynski, Daniel	Technomania	Techno
Levi Dexter	Rockabilly Idol	Rockabilly
UL Cease	The Wonderful World of Cease a Leo	Hip Hop
Lins, Ivan	Live at MC6	Jazz
Longview	High Lonesome	Bluegrass
**Lopez, Jennifer	On the 6	Pop
Lost Goat	Equator	Rock
Lunachicks	Luxury Problem	Punk/alternative
Marnie	Legitimo Polvo	Dance/Leftfield
Megace	Inner War	Rock
Melody, Sandra & Troublesome	Scrubbs	Reggae
Milsap, Ronnie	Pure Love/A Legend in my Time	Country/Rock
Moksha	Mindwork 97-99	Trance
Monroe, Bill	Live from Mountain Stage	Bluegrass
Moonlight String Orchestra	Plays the Music of Barbara Streisand	MOR/Class X
Moonlight String Orchestra	Plays the Music of Whitney Houston	MOR/Class X

Since the 1950s, different pop music genres have developed, finding favour with a range of youth groups and cultures. These include mods and hippies in the 1960s and punks in the 1970s. Reggae music is one example with its roots in AfroCaribbean culture.

The music is recognizable by its emphasis on a slow rhythmic offbeat (provided by the bass). The music is also closely tied to the Rastafarian religion in both the lyrics and the performers' style (dreadlocks and so on, as exemplified by Bob Marley – see Figure 5.4).

Source 5.6a Public Enemy

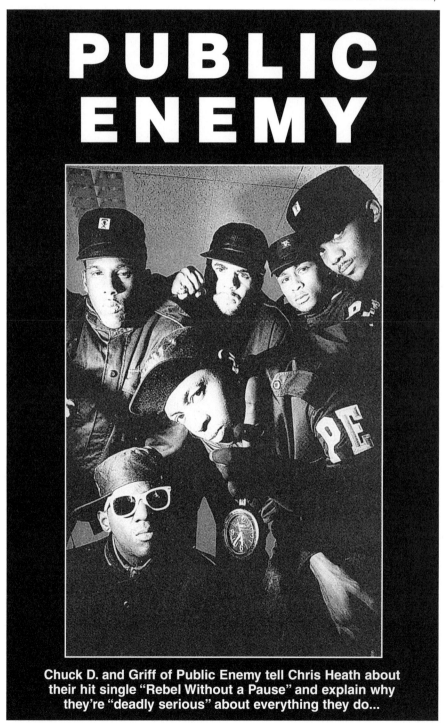

Chuck D. and Griff of Public Enemy tell Chris Heath about their hit single "Rebel Without a Pause" and explain why they're "deadly serious" about everything they do...

Sources 5.6 a–d

Try to identify which genre of music is linked to each picture. Give reasons for your choices.

ACTIVITY

Choose one genre of pop music and describe:

• its distinctive musical sound, style and lyrics;

• the typical singers/groups who produce the music;

• where and when the music is most often produced and consumed.

Source 5.6c (Kerrang Spotlight, 3 October 1987)

Source 5.6b The Damned

Figure 5.4

Source 5.6d

GENRE DEVELOPMENT

As mentioned earlier in this chapter, genres rarely stay the same. One reason for this is audience need. A popular formula is unlikely to stay popular if it becomes too predictable. Also, new producers and writers will tend to add fresh ingredients by way of new situations, characters or even new technology, as in science fiction.

Many of the themes of genres reflect wider social changes. For example, gangster films made in the 1930s dealt with the activities of gangs involved in bootleg liquor during prohibition in the USA. The films were often based on actual gangsters' lives, such as Al Capone, or events like the St Valentine's Day Massacre. As America moved into the Depression of the 1930s, and social research began to reveal how crime was bred by urban deprivation, there appeared a cycle of films looking at gangsters' social backgrounds and how they became gangsters. An example is *Angels with Dirty Faces*. Although in many post-war Hollywood films it appeared as though organized crime was a thing of the past, by the early 1970s it was increasingly clear that, in fact, its influence was greater than ever. Films such as *The Godfather* reflected the success and respectability achieved by the modern Mafia in America and Italy.

CASE STUDY: TELEVISION POLICE SERIES

For the past 40 years there has been a variety of police series on television. Drama centred on crime has been consistently successful in achieving good audience ratings. Each decade has seen new series that have 'broken the mould' by introducing new elements to the genre. Some of these changes reflect developments in technology. When *Dixon of Dock Green* was originally broadcast in the 1950s, most of the filming took place live in brightly lit studios, using cumbersome, heavy cameras and overhead microphones. By the 1990s, filming could take place on location, using lightweight mobile cameras, sophisticated microphones and recording on to video or film to be edited in post production. These technical advances have enabled a stronger sense of realism to be achieved, in some series resembling documentary (see Figure 5.5).

Aside from technology, the main reason for television police series having changed is the need to respond to wider developments in society in terms of changes in policing and the public's views of the police. The neighbourhood 'bobby on the beat' as represented by *Dixon of Dock Green* would not be so readily accepted today because not only is it uncharacteristic of modern urban policing, but also the public is now more sceptical and would not believe in the kind of idealized and 'pure' police character that Sergeant Dixon seemed to represent. Another change reflected in television police series is the increasing presence of women in the police force. This was acknowledged, for example, in Britain in the 1970s series *Juliet Bravo* and in America during the 1980s with *Cagney and Lacey*.

> ### Sources 5.7 a–e
>
> 1 How have television police series changed since *Dixon of Dock Green*?
> 2 How do British police series compare with American ones?

Figure 5.5 (*The Bill*)

Dixon of Dock Green – a cluster of values

The character of George Dixon is never far removed from the centre of the action and his shadow is cast throughout the narrative.

Like the classic boy scout, Dixon was shown to be loyal, honest, trustworthy and brave. He was hard-working, dedicated, punctual, reliable, strong but never violent, forceful but not domineering, knowledgeable and helpful. The different facets of the character were developed in scenes with his superiors – whom he treated with due respect and humour; his colleagues – whom he worked with; younger policeman – whom he helped with care, concern and the benefit of his experience; the public – whom he worked for and who knew him as he knew them; and the villains – again people he knew and who came quietly, submitting to Dixon's authority.

This vouches for Dixon's position as part of the community; not only does he work with them, but he lives amongst them. His experience is not that of a visiting policeman but of a member of the community; a neighbour and a friend.

Source 5.7a

The Sweeney – the key word is action

The series represented the pinnacle of the development of 'Action' in the British police series. The 'Action' series as they came to be known were heavily influenced by a stream of American films in the late 1960s which all featured a rogue cop as the central character – *Dirty Harry* (1971), *Magnum Force, Madigan* (1968), and *The New Centurions* – and the American television series which these influenced – *Kojak* (1973), *Starsky and Hutch* (1975), and other imitations too numerous to mention where the heroes were all on the borders of respectability. In these shows the concern for detail was overshadowed by the demand for action – movement, pace and violence synthesized with the sound track to produce the maximum effect. Many of the shows had greater flexibility in the camera work than the actors, with a constant search for new angles, new uses of slow motion and stop frame filming to heighten the action. Car chases had been around a long time – there is even one in *The Blue Lamp*! – but in these shows they became obligatory, a very firmly established convention of the genre.

Source 5.7b

The Bill – individualism

The emphasis on individuals traits, the domestic situations and the career progression of the main characters – especially the female characters – presents a different picture of individualism to that developed in *The Sweeney*.

The Bill demonstrates this most effectively, with a return to the fictional roots of the police series at a small London police station and the construction of a realistic environment for the routine police drama.

It retains enough of the drama of the major crimes, with the CID section located within the same building, and by interweaving story lines – similar to the five-story narrative developed by *Hill Street Blues* in the American context – allowing for both sides of the police role to be depicted.

There is no challenge to the central thrust of the police series, portraying the Sun Hill station as honest, hardworking, diligent but troubled officers.

Source 5.7c (A Clarke, *Popular Media Culture*)

Heartbeat

Police Constable Nick Rowan and his recently qualified doctor wife, Kate, turn their backs on a hectic London lifestyle, pack their bags and head North for the Yorkshire moorlands where Kate was born, and the little village of Aidensfield.

From now on Aidensfield's neat Yorkstone police house will be their home, and PC Nick Rowan the village 'bobby'.

This is his patch.

The good life it may be, far from the frenetic streets of London, but if Nick and Kate think they are in for a rural backwater existence, they are soon to have their eyes well and truly opened.

For this is 1964, the eve of the 'Swinging 60s' when Britain led the world in an explosion of music, fashion, trends and, above all, a revolution in the attitudes of society itself.

The rapes and robberies, muggings and murder of the Metropolis may not be too much in evidence in Aidensfield, but Nick and Kate soon find themselves fully occupied with the trials and tribulations of village life twenty-four hours a day.

For 'living over the shop' offers no respite. Escape for a country copper is out of the question; he's available to all day and night.

As Sergeant Blaketon acidly points out to Kate at their first meeting, 'If he's here, he's on duty.'

Nick is attached to the police station in the market town of Ashfordly, where Blaketon is his suspicious, humourless and charmless section sergeant.

Source 5.7d (Yorkshire TV)

The Cops

The Cops subverts the television police series as we have come to know it. Filmed in a pseudo-documentary style, there are no heroes. Officers are flawed, often unpleasant and frequently brutal as they dole out their own brand of summary justice. They deal with life at the sharp end of policing, fighting a losing battle to bring order to poverty-ridden sink estates, the places where people no one knows what to do with are regularly dumped. These cops do not solve picturesque murders over pints of real ale. They deal with the maggot-ridden, fly-blown reality of death.

Real police are furious at the depiction of a group of fictional officers who are driven by personal vendettas and sexual voraciousness, and abuse their uniform in order to settle scores, often with each other.

Source 5.7e (*Radio Times*, 24-30 October 1999)

ACTIVITY

Compare and contrast two episodes of television police series (past or present) with respect to the following:

- *opening and closing titles/credits sequences*
  use of music, identification of setting and so on;
- *setting*
  locations used, time of day, lighting, and so on;
- *characters*
  main police characters, villains, minor characters;
  representations of gender, ethnicity, class;
  with whom is the audience meant to identify?

- *narrative*
  conflict and resolution;
  hierarchy of plots;
  law and order themes;
- *style*
  camerawork;
  editing;
  music;
- *conclusion*
  how are the police represented overall (sympathetically, critically etc)? What degree of realism is achieved? Is the context of production and transmission significant (who made the series, when it has been scheduled, which channel)?

6 ┃ AUDIENCE

Street-wise is out – media-wise is in

Figure 6.1 (*Times Educational Supplement*, 3 October 1986)

WHO IS THE AUDIENCE?

Audience size

The term 'mass media' suggests large audiences. The exact size of audiences is revealed by surveys and sales figures regularly produced by media organizations.

Television

The Broadcasters' Audience Research Board (BARB) produces information concerning the number of viewers for individual programmes. It does this by issuing a representative sample of viewers with meters that record when their television is on, which channel and programme are being shown, and whether or not anyone is actually present in the room (recorded by individual push buttons on a handset). This data provides the basis for the much-publicized weekly **TV ratings** (TVR).

Source 6.1 National top 50

1 Which programme types, or genres, appear to be the most popular?
2 Much has been made of the tendency of viewers to stay with one channel all evening, or for a programme that follows a very popular one to inherit its audience. Is there any evidence to support this?
3 How do BBC2 and Channel 4 achieve good ratings?

Channel	Average weekly viewing (Hours: mins) per person	Share of total viewing %	% Reach average daily	% Reach average weekly
All/any TV	26:45	100.0	78.6	94.6
BBC 1 (incl. Breakfast News)	7:14	27.0	61.2	89.9
BBC 2	2:47	10.4	38.5	79.6
Total/any BBC	10:01	37.4	66.8	91.4
ITV (inc. GMTV)	8:20	31.2	60.1	89.4
CHANNEL 4/S4C	2:51	10.6	39.1	79.0
CHANNEL 5	1:34	5.9	20.2	48.5
Total/any commercial terrestrial TV	12:45	47.7	68.2	92.0
Other viewing (cable/satellite)	3:59	14.9	20.6	30.8

Hours of viewing, share of audience and reach (including timeshift)
Week ending 31 October 1999

Figure 6.2 (*BARB* 31 October 1999)

Top 40 BBC1 and ITV

	Title	Day	Start	Viewers (millions)	% Change (week)	Broadcaster/ producer	Last year
1	Coronation Street	Mon	1932	15.91	0.2	ITV/Grandada	1
2	Coronation Street	Sun	1930	14.38	-7.3	ITV/Granada	3
3	Who Wants/Millionaire?	Mon	2002	13.59	12.0	ITV/Celador	-
4	Coronation Street	Wed	2151	13.40	-15.0	ITV/Granada	4
5	Who Wants/Millionaire?	Wed	2223	13.24	0.3	ITV/Celador	-
6	Eastenders	Tue	1930	13.10	2.5	BBC1	5
7	Who Wants/Millionaire?	Tue	2000	12.97	-0.1	ITV/Celador	-
8	Coronation Street	Fri	1931	12.61	-4.0	ITV/Granada	2
9	Who Wants/Millionaire?	Thur	2002	12.33	2.4	ITV/Celador	-
10	Emmerdale	Tue	1901	11.44	3.2	ITV/Yorkshire	8
11	Emmerdale	Wed	1859	11.38	-6.2	ITV/Yorkshire	-
12	Eastenders	Thur	1931	11.33	18.0	BBC1	6
13	Touch of Frost	Sun	2002	10.62		ITV/Yorkshire	-
14	Emmerdale	Thur	1902	10.25	-17.0	ITV/Yorkshire	13
15	Eastenders	Mon	2000	10.21	-9.0	BBC1	7
16	Stars in their Eyes	Sat	2015	9.79	-2.0	ITV/Granada	11
17	Bad Girls	Tue	2101	9.44		ITV/Shed	-
18	Monsignor Renard	Mon	2102	9.15	-13.0	ITV/Carlton	-
19	Ground Force	Fri	1959	9.05	-3.0	BBC/Bazal	17
20	Blind Date	Sat	1915	8.98	2.0	ITV/LWT	26
21	2000 Grand National	Sat	1545	8.94		BBC1	14
22	Big Match/Champ League	Wed	1931	8.75		ITV/ISN	9
23	Antiques Roadshow	Sun	1845	8.55	-2.0	BBC1	-
24	Always & Everyone	Thur	2101	8.09	-0.1	ITV/Granada	-
25	My Kind of Music	Fri	2001	8.06	-6.0	ITV/LWT	-
26	A Question of Sport	Mon	1900	8.03	12.0	BBC1	-
27	Monarch of the Glen	Sun	2000	7.98	-1.5	BBC1 Ecosse	-
28	Celeb/Ready Steady Cook	Wed	1929	7.49		BBC1/Bazal	-
29	Airport	Tue	1959	7.38	-7.5	BBC1	-
30	News and Weather	Sun	2050	7.35	-7.0	BBC!	-
31	You've been Framed	Sat	1831	7.28	-9.0	ITV/Granada	-
32	Last of the Summer Wine	Sun	1815	7.27	-8.0	BBC!	-
33	Deceit	Sun	2102	7.19	-4.0	BBC1	-
34	Wish you were here ..?	Mon	1901	6.79	-6.0	ITV/Central	-
35	Beware – Thieves at Work	Fri	2102	6.68		ITV/LWT	-
36	Big Match/Champ League	Tue	2202	6.46		ITV	-
37	Brian Conley Show	Sat	2104	6.44	-2.5	ITV/Thames	-
38	Holiday	Tue	1900	6.31	6.2	BBC1	40
39	News	Mon	1800	6.28	3.4	BBC1	-
40	News	Tue	1800	6.28	0.3	BBC1	34

Top 20 BBC2 and Channel 4

	Title	Day	Start	Viewers (M)	Channel	Last week
1	Gardeners World	Fri	2030	4.19	BBC2	1
2	The Simpsons	Mon	1801	3.95	BBC2	6
3	Friends	Fri	2100	3.87	C4	21
4	The Simpsons	Fri	1820	3.47	BBC2	2
5	Countdown	Mon	1630	3.43	C4	4
6	Journeys/Bottom/Sea	Mon	2100	3.36	BBC2	3
7	Frasier	Fri	2200	3.36	C4	31
8	Countdown	Tue	1630	3.32	C4	5
9	Home Front	Wed	2000	3.30	BBC2	17
10	Countdown	Fri	1630	3.27	C4	11
11	Da Ali G Show	Fri	2235	3.24	C4	9
12	Greece Uncovered	Fri	2315	3.17	C4	36
13	Have I Got News For You	Mon	2200	3.09	BBC2	20
14	Robot Wars	Fri	1845	3.07	BBC2	8
15	ER	Wed	2100	3.04	C4	14
16	Countdown	Thur	1630	3.02	C4	10
17	Farscape	Mon	1825	3.01	BBC2	27
18	The Simpsons	Fri	1800	2.96	BBC2	7
19	Countdown	Wed	1630	2.92	C4	12
20	Top Tens	Sat	2100	2.73	C4	58

Source 6.1 *Broadcast* TV Ratings week ending 9 April 2000

Radio

Radio listening is measured by Radio Joint Audience Research Limited (RAJAR) on the basis of diaries filled in each week by a representative sample of British households. All stations listened to for at least five minutes are noted. After declining for many years in the face of competition from television, radio listening has now stabilized. This is no doubt related to the steady expansion in the choice of services available to the audience.

Radio listening (June – September 1999)

Radio Station	Average hours per listener	% share of listening
All radio	23.2	100
All BBC	16.2	50.3
BBC Radio 1	9.3	10.6
Radio 2	12.7	12.2
Radio 3	6.3	1.2
Radio 4	11.9	10.6
Radio 5	7.4	4.2
Local/regional	11.5	11.4
All commercial	15.4	47.8
National commercial		
Classic FM	7.2	4.1
Talk Radio	7.7	1.5
Virgin Radio	6.9	2.2
Atlantic 252	4.9	0.9
All local commercial	14.9	39.2
Other listening	7.5	1.9

Figure 6.3 (*Radio Listening*, RAJAR)

Note: Radio is listened to, on average, by 90 per cent of the population each week in Britain.

Press/magazines

Circulation figures of newspapers and magazines are measured by the Audit Bureau of Circulation (ABC). Research on readership – how many readers see an individual copy of a newspaper or magazine – is conducted by the National Readership Survey (NRS). Newspapers average above three readers per copy, whereas magazines can be many more, depending on cost, reference information and so on.

Top-selling consumer magazines 1999

	Title	Publisher	Average Net Circulation per issue		Title	Publisher	Average Net Circulation per issue
1	What's on TV	IPC tx	1,813,784	51	B	Attic Futura	235,941
2	Radio Times	BBC Worldwide UK	1,390,481	52	Family Circle	IPC SouthBank	231,783
3	Reader's Digest	Reader's Digest Association	1,275,592	53	Smash Hits	Emap Elan	230,764
4	Take a Break	H Bauer	1,255,832	54	SW – Slimming World – The Magazine	SW – The Magazine	228,111
5	TV Times	IPC tx	825,760	55	Viz	John Brown Publishing	226,869
6	TV Quick	H Bauer	725,795	56	Men's Health	Rodale Press	218,724
7	FHM	Emap Metro	701,089	57	Teletubbies	BBC Worldwide UK	206,791
8	Woman	IPC Connect	686,169	58	Q	Emap Elan	204,516
9	Woman's Own	IPC Connect	597,179	59	She	National Magazine Company	211,031
10	Bella	H Bauer	585,295	60	Elle (UK)	Emap Elan	205,151
11	Woman's Weekly	IPC Connect	567,091	61	Toybox	BBC Worldwide UK	200,961
12	That's Life	H Bauer	521,223	62	Loot (National, Group Certificate)	Loot	198,097
13	Chat	IPC Connect	502,364	63	BBC Homes & Antiques	BBC Worldwide UK	205,329
14	Hello!	Hello!	493,322	64	TV & Satellite Week	IPC tx	198,651
15	Prima	G&J	485,580	65	Rosemary Conley Diet & Fitness	Quorn House Publishing	190,225
16	Cosmopolitan	National Magazine Company	470,142	66	Private Eye	Pressdram	184,622
17	Best	G&J	467.330	67	Woman's Realm	IPC Connect	182,609
18	Saga Magazine	Saga Publishing	935,399	68	Vogue	Condé Nast	200,462
19	Candis	Newhall Publications	449,754	69	Weekly News	DC Thomson	177,326
20	Marie Claire	IPC SouthBank Publishing Company	437,642	70	Maxpower	Emap Active	176,110
21	Sugar	Attic Futura	431,394	71	Computer Shopping	Dennis Publishing	173,256
22	People's Friend	DC Thomson	427,786	72	Your Home	G&J	173,813
23	OK!	Northern & Shell	413,148	73	Top Santé Health & Bauty	Emap Elan	170,131
24	National Geographic	National Geographic Society	411,089	74	Top Gear	BBC Worldwide UK	182,542
25	Now	IPC Connect	386,383	75	Garden Answers	Emap Active	167,245
26	Top of the Pops	BBC Worldwide UK	385,441	76	Country Living	National Magazine Company	163,520
27	Official Playstation Magazine	Future	385,764	77	Homes & Ideas	IPC SouthBank	162,349
28	Sainsbury's: The Magazine	New Crane Publishing	385,061	78	Red	Emap Elan	170,101
29	BBC Gardeners' World	BBC Worldwide UK	380,559	79	19	IPC SouthBank	160,237
30	Loaded	IPC Music & Sport	384,351	80	Live & Kicking	BBC Worldwide UK	156,707
31	Auto Trader (national)	Auto Trader	372,029	81	PC Pro	Dennis Publishing	155,184
32	Good Housekeeping	National Magazine Company	370,436	82	Homes & Gardens	IPC SouthBank	168,732
33	My Weekly	DC Thomson	350,921	83	What Car?	Haymarket Motoring Publications	154,192
34	The Economist (worldwide excluding America)	The Economist News	375,356	84	Empire	Emap Metro	151,348
35	It's Bliss	Emap Elan	310,389	85	Mizz	IPC SouthBank	150,230
36	Yours	Choice Publications	310,054	86	Teletubbies Special	BBC Worldwide UK	143,599
37	Maxim	Dennis Publishing	310,096	87	Personal Computer World	VNU Business Publications	141,746
38	More!	Emap Elan	293,471	88	Shout	DC Thomson	140,618
39	Diamond Free ads (Supermart Group)	Freead Mart	292,805	89	GQ	Condé Nast	145,144
40	Woman & Home	IPC SouthBank Publishing Company	293,847	90	Front	Cabal Communications	140,154
41	Essentials	IPC SouthBank Publishing Company	290,542	91	House & Garden	Condé Nast	160,831
42	New Woman	Emap Elan	273,016	92	BBC Good Homes	BBC Worldwide UK	145,283
43	The Big Issue (national group)	Big Issue	258,956	93	Looks	Emap Elan	131,044
44	Inside Soap	Attic Futura	251,867	94	The Real Homes Magazine	Cabal Communications	130,084
45	BBC Good Food	BBC Worldwide UK	290,646	95	New Scientist	Reed Business Information	132,799
46	Company	National Magazine Company	242,087	96	Minx	Emap Elan	126,883
47	TV Hits	Attic Futura	241,746	97	PC Plus	Future Publishing	126,815
48	J-17	Emap Elan	238,382	98	The Economist (Continental Europe)	The Economist News	152,205
49	Ideal Home	IPC SouthBank Publishing Company	237,734	99	Loot (South East, Group Certificate)	Loot	124,643
50	House Beautiful	National Magazine Company	252,124	100	The Big Issue	Big Issue	123,890

Source 6.2 (*PPA ABC*, 1999)

Refering to Source 6.2, produce a
chart (pie or bar) illustrating the main
areas of interest of magazine readers,
such as women's magazines, music,
motoring and so on. To reflect total
numbers, you will need to make some
rough calculations.

Cinema

Despite the rise of video as a format for
viewing films, cinema attendance has
steadily risen since 1985.

Whether or not this can be sustained
in the future is open to question, as
more people acquire widescreen
televisions on which they can view films
chosen virtually on demand (if they
subscribe to digital film channels or
British Telecom's dial-a-video service
due to be introduced in the near future).

	UK Cinema screens and admissions	
Year	**Total screens**	**Admissions (millions)**
1948	4700	1900
1958	4000	830
1968	1700	260
1978	1550	95
1988	1350	90
1993	1850	106
1994	1900	117
1995	1990	108
1996	2100	124
1997	2200	140
1998	2450	136

Source 6.3

Source 6.3

1 What factors help to explain the
decline in cinema attendances
between 1948 and 1998?
2 Why do you think cinema
attendances have risen in the past
decade?

Pop music

With the arrival of the compact disc in the early 1980s, vinyl steadily declined as a format on which to record music. It is now largely confined to the dance market. After a long period of falling sales, the single has bounced back in the past few years. This is mainly due to its popularity among the pre-teen audience of boy and girl groups, such as the Spice Girls, Steps and Westlife.

Daily patterns of media use

Sources 6.4a and b

1 How might patterns of media usage differ at the weekend?
2 What seasonal variations may occur?

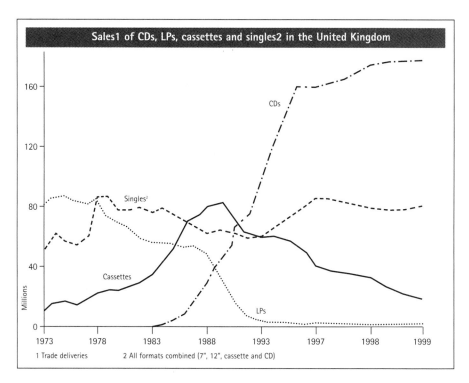

Figure 6.4 (*BPI*)

Source 6.4a (Jeremy Tunstall, *The Media in Britain*, Constable, 1983)

ACTIVITY

To test how much the patterns of media usage described in Sources 6.4 and 6.5 still apply today, conduct your own survey. This should ask a representative sample of people (20–30) to make a diary of their own media usage during the week. To be able to compare age groups, ensure you ask equal groups of those aged 5–15, 16–25, 26–55, 56+.

How much have new technologies, such as the Internet and video games, changed the situation?

" Jeremy Tunstall's account is based on various media audience surveys.

Time of day or year greatly influences the kind of audience for radio. On weekdays, breakfast and driving-to-work give radio its peak audiences from 7am to 8.30am; the other early morning medium is newspapers. During the day there is a continuing lower-level use of newspapers and radio, both with housewives at home and with men and women at work. The midday meal break marks a small new blip in (morning) newspaper reading and in radio; it also marks the start of a significant audience for television. The afternoon sees a continuing decline in the radio audience, as television programming starts to attract audiences initially of housewives and retired people, but then of children returning from school.

In the early evening all the media battle it out together, not only with each other but with other activities such as preparing and eating food. At any time in the early evening fewer men are home, but of people already home a bigger proportion of men devote their prime attention to television. Around 6pm many Britons are eating, the radio is beginning its final descent into an evening of negligible audiences, while the television audience is already large. Around 6 to 7pm evening newspapers get their main readers, but morning newspapers are still being read. The majority of the evening television audience cue their viewing with a newspaper TV schedule. As the evening progresses some young people watch television and increasingly large proportions also give it their main attention. Television hits its peak audience around 9pm, and the 'truce' which ends at this hour is realistic in that fairly few children under ten years continue to view. The adult TV audience declines sharply after 10pm, and there is a small increase in the radio audience around 11pm as people go to bed.

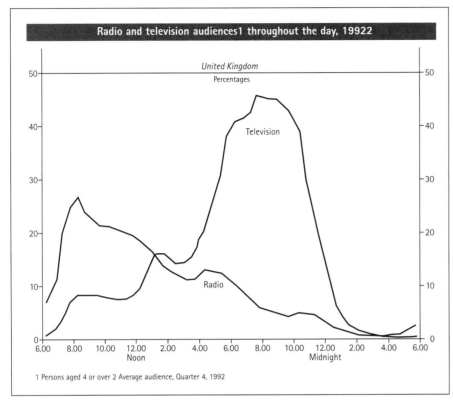

Radio and television audiences1 throughout the day, 19922

United Kingdom
Percentages

Television

Radio

6.00 | 8.00 | 10.00 | 12.00 Noon | 2.00 | 4.00 | 6.00 | 8.00 | 10.00 | 12.00 Midnight | 2.00 | 4.00 | 6.00

1 Persons aged 4 or over 2 Average audience, Quarter 4, 1992

Source 6.4b (BARB, RAJAR, AGB Limited, RSL Limited)

Children's favourite medium is television and those aged 5–15 are especially heavy viewers. Heaviest viewers of all are boys aged 15 or under – possibly because girls do more household chores. At 16 this changes radically. The 16+ age groups are the lightest viewers of television – because they are often outside the home, or certainly the sitting room. They are the heaviest users of radio, records and cinema films. The 16+ age group are especially irregular buyers of papers; but they do read newspapers and buy magazines, often age-specific ones.

Somewhere in the early twenties, and typically at the point of marriage, all this changes again. It is only at marriage – or setting up housekeeping – that Britons start both to buy and to read a daily paper; television viewing increases, and cinema attendance virtually ends – especially after the birth of the first child. People in their forties are typically quite heavy users for all the stay-at-home media; television, radio and newspapers.

People around the age of 60 are especially heavy readers of newspapers, but this drops off sharply after 65. Radio listening also declines. Elderly people are also heavy television viewers (especially ITV). This heavy TV diet is a reversion back towards the youth pattern in another sense; while old people dislike youth culture and its music, they like children's television - substantial proportions of whose audience is old people viewing without a child present. Elderly people are great complainers about such things as excessive violence, explicit sex and lack of respect for authority; such attitudes probably partly explain their liking for children's programming.

Source 6.5 (Jeremy Tunstall, *The Media in Britain*, Constable, 1983)

Social composition of audiences

The advert in Figure 6.5 appeared in *Campaign*, a magazine for the advertising industry. It reflects the point that advertisers are usually intent on reaching or **targeting** a specific audience in terms of social composition. The three main factors are all included here: age, class and gender. Those with the most money to spend on advertised goods are aged 15–44, middle-class (ABC1 – see Figure 6.5) and female (women are responsible for about four-fifths of the purchases of domestic consumer goods), hence the greater number of media products aimed at such groups.

If advertisers can target the audiences most likely to buy their products, then they will avoid wasting money on audiences unlikely to purchase their goods such as those who are too poor. An organization that helps advertisers target audiences is the British Market Research Bureau. The BMRB surveys over 24,000 people each year, asking about their spending, lifestyle and media exposure in order to produce a **Target Group Index**. This can be used by advertisers to find out where best to place adverts. For example, BMW cars are not going to want to reach *The Sun's* readers, who are mainly working class and unable to afford such cars.

Figure 6.5 (*Campaign*, 10
April 1987)

HIGH PROFILE

THE VALUE

The Times has a higher percentage
of ABC1 women aged 15–44* than any
other quality daily newspaper.

Furthermore, The Times is the most
cost effective quality daily newspaper
for reaching ABC1 women aged under 45.

So if you're looking to raise your
profile among young upmarket women,
why pay more for less?

You simply can't afford to miss
The Times off your schedule.

Telephone 01-833-7132 and ask for
Jacquie Griffith-Jones.

THE ☙❧ TIMES
quality at the right price

Figure 6.6

Social class

The means of identification used in advertising is 'social grade'. This is a classification based on the occupation of the head of the household, and it indicates the household's spending power. The list below shows the social grades, the occupation to which they refer, and the approximate proportions (in percentages) of each grade in the total UK population.

A	Higher-level managerial, administrative and professional	4%
B	Intermediate managerial, administrative and professional	15%
C1	Supervisory or clerical and junior managerial, administrative and professional	34%
C2	Skilled manual	21%
D	Semi-skilled and unskilled manual	19%
E	Casual labourers, State pensioners and the unemployed	6%

Source 6.6 (*National Readership Survey*)

Daily Newspapers	Total	Sex		Social grade		Age		
		men	women	ABC1	C2DE	15–24	35–44	55–64
The Sun	21.0	24.0	18.0	13.3	28.4	27.7	21.0	18.6
Daily Mirror	13.6	14.9	12.4	8.9	18.2	13.7	12.2	16.5
Daily Record	3.8	3.9	3.6	2.6	4.9	3.7	4.1	4.3
Daily Star	3.5	5.0	2.1	1.9	5.1	5.3	4.1	2.4
Daily Mail	12.2	12.6	11.9	16.1	8.6	8.3	11.7	16.3
Daily Express	5.1	5.5	4.7	6.1	4.0	3.5	4.7	6.9
Daily Telegraph	5.2	5.9	4.6	8.9	1.6	3.7	4.3	7.9
The Times	4.0	5.1	3.0	7.0	1.1	3.9	4.6	4.1
The Guardian	2.3	2.6	2.1	4.2	0.6	2.3	2.5	2.2
The Independent	1.2	1.4	1.0	2.1	0.4	1.2	1.7	1.1
Financial Times	1.3	2.0	0.7	2.4	0.3	0.8	1.9	1.1
Any daily newspaper	56	61	52	55	56	52	52	60

Readership of national daily newspapers by sex, social class and age 1999 (percentage of adults)

Source 6.6

Work out which newspapers have the highest proportion of readers who are:

(a) middle class (ABC1);
(b) working class (C2DE);
(c) male;
(d) female;
(e) 15 – 44;
(f) 45+.

Try to confirm your conclusions by examining the adverts in each newspaper (especially for jobs).

Although television is rather crude for targeting specific audiences, there is an increasing ability to do so as different programmes appeal to particular types of viewer. This may reflect the time of day – for example mid-morning programmes capturing a high proportion of female and older viewers at home or late night weekend programmes being seen by young single adults and teenagers. Furthermore, programmes, or even channels (on satellite and cable), may be geared to subjects such as sport or travel as they might attract advertisers for such products.

Radio has a much greater capacity for reaching audiences targeted by advertisers, with its growing tendency to offer specialized programming (such as Classic FM and Virgin).

ACTIVITIES

1 By listing the adverts that appear within different television programmes (at varying times of day) on ITV and Channel 4, see if there is any pattern that indicates a target audience for that programme (in terms of age, gender, class, lifestyle, and so on).
2 Conduct a small social survey of radio listening by asking a sample (20 – 30 people) of differing ages and gender to identify their preferred radio stations. From your results, see if there are patterns that reveal the social profile of the typical listener for particular radio stations.

Figure 6.7 (*Music Week,* 9 April 1994)

CAMPAIGN OF THE WEEK

ROXETTE
CRASH! BOOM! BANG!

With **Roxette**'s single Sleeping In My Car already riding high in the charts, EMI is targeting pop fans rather than serious musos with its marketing campaign for Crash! Boom! Bang!, the band's new album which is released on Monday.

Record label: EMI

Media agencies/executives: London Media – press; TMD Carat – TV/Jen Parker and Martin James – London Media.

Marketing manager: Jonathan Green.

TV: There will be a one-week national co-op campaign on ITV (with Our Price) plus solus advertising for one week in the Scotland, Grampian and Granada ITV regions.

Press: Ads will run in *Smash Hits* aimed at teenage buyers.

Posters: There will be a nationwide co-op campaign (with HMV) and 48-sheet sites in London, Birmingham, Glasgow and Sheffield.

In-store: Selected independents and all of the multiples including Woolworths, Our Price, Virgin, Tower, HMV and Menzies will run in-store and window displays.

Target audience: 14- to 34-year-olds with no particular male or female bias.

ACTIVITIES

Advertising campaign

1 Choose a product that is used by a large number of people.

2 Identify which types of people are most likely to buy the product – that is, the **target audience.** Consider:

   (a) their ages – 15–24, 25–44 and so on;

   (b) their class – ABC1, C2DE;

   (c) their gender – male or female.

3 Identify which branches of the media would be most appropriate for advertising your product. Consider:

   (a) how to reach your target audience (which media do they consume most?) – try to give specific examples of newspapers read or TV programmes watched;

   (b) the advantages or disadvantages of the medium in question, such as the size of the audience, attention and so on.

4 Work out how you are going to advertise your product in one of the media and provide details in the form of a TV treatment, an outline of a radio script or a rough sketch for a magazine ad with brief details. (You might find it helpful to examine existing approaches adopted by advertising agencies – but resist the temptation merely to copy their strategies.)

Minority audiences

Where production costs are low, and there is little dependence on advertising revenue, smaller 'minority' audiences may be catered for (as discussed in Chapter 3 with reference to radio, publishing and music). Popular music is a case where the audience has become increasingly fragmented, so that the top 20 singles or LPs no longer reflect the range of musical interest of audiences.

ACTIVITY

Select one genre of popular music – reggae, heavy metal for example – and try to find out the nature of the audience.

1 How large is it?

2 What is its social profile in terms of age, gender, class or ethnic origin?

3 How is the audience kept informed about the music if it is poorly represented on national radio and television, or in the best-selling music papers/magazines?

To answer these questions will require tracking down specialist music magazines, or finding an audience sample to interview.

Gaps in the market

From the commercial point of view, identifying gaps in the market means identifying audiences with purchasing power whose needs are not currently being satisfied. The launch of new newspapers and magazines is nearly always based on such gaps being recognized.

£1.50 FIRST ISSUE
Later
SUCCESS MONEY WOMEN

ESCAPE!
How four men quit
their jobs and got rich

**Sex tips we tried on
our own girlfriends**

Be fitter at 30 than 20

'She's an old trollop'
Vinnie Jones: Agony uncle

Rollerball!
James Caan on the ultimate
cinema bloodsport

When girlfriends attack!
Don't let her jealousy ruin your life

SPECIAL REPORT
GUNS, TORTURE, DANCING
The truth behind the Summer of Love

Later
with our
covergirl...
page 40

OH, AND...,
DVD explained, Robert Harris,
James Coburn on Bruce Lee,
become a rich landlord

Source 6.7a

minx
October 1996

SPECIAL PRICE £1

Bonkers
couples who
do it every night

Out of it
models on heroin

Loafing with
George Clooney,
the *Friends* girls

Good call
how to be a
phone pest

**Smart
new
magazine!**

35
*pages of
fashion &
beauty*

FOR girls with a lust for life

Source 6.7b

FOR MEN WHO ARE GROWING UP

the reader

He is in his late 20s or early 30s. He is at the time of his
life when ...

- his motivation for work has changed and his job has now become a career.
- the barometer for his success is no longer based on his ability to drink six pints
  on a Monday lunchtime.
- his girlfriend is now his long-term partner.
- he now co-owns or is about to buy a home with his girlfriend.
- he takes time making serious decisions as each one will tend to have long-
  term consequences later on in his life.
- he is starting to enjoy the finer things in life.
- he takes taxis instead of tubes or buses.
- he is dining at restaurants and entertaining at home.
- he is looking for a magazine that reflects his changing lifestyle, a magazine
  that realises that he has reached the most challenging yet potentially most
  prosperous and fulfilling period of his life. He knows the difference between
  Pinotage and a Pinot Noir.

***Later* will provide him with the information he needs to
face the challenges that lie ahead. It will reassure him
that the fun's not over but that the food, the clothes,
the cars, the sex and every other aspect of adult life is
superior ...**

Source 6.7c

Emap Elan
spotted a gap
in the market
for a magazine
aimed at young
women that has
humour and is
different from
the rest of the
market.
*Women's glossy
and youth
magazines
(median ages)*

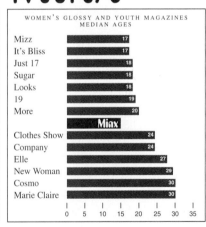

WOMEN'S GLOSSY AND YOUTH MAGAZINES
MEDIAN AGES

Magazine	Median age
Mizz	17
It's Bliss	17
Just 17	18
Sugar	18
Looks	18
19	19
More	20
Minx	
Clothes Show	24
Company	24
Elle	27
New Woman	29
Cosmo	30
Marie Claire	30

(scale: 0 5 10 15 20 25 30 35)

Who is the **MINX** reader?

The Minx reader is in her early to mid-twenties, intelligent and
fun-loving.
With her Walkman tuned into Oasis, she'll be shopping at
Kookai or French Connection, drinking Sea Breezes and
wishing she worked on *ER*, lived with *Friends* and hung out at
Cheers.
She's Danni Behr, she's Patsy Kensit, she's as comfortable in
trainers as she is in Patrick Cox loafers.
In addition to reading her favourite magazine, she may pick up
a book or a broadsheet as well. She earns and enjoys her own
money and has a definite lust for life.
She enjoys her sex life but believes in her relationship.

Source 6.7d

Using sources 6.7 a, b, c and d to give you an idea of the kinds of things to look for, try to spot a gap in the magazine market by identifying an audience/readership for which no magazine currently caters. It may be a new activity or interest or a broader lifestyle that is being neglected. It might be that you think the existing magazines are inadequate or unsuccessful in meeting their readers' needs.

Present your ideas in the form of a proposal in which you clearly define your target audience and present your evidence that: (a) there is an audience for your proposed magazine; and (b) no existing magazine effectively caters for this audience.

ADDRESSING THE AUDIENCE

Communication via the media rarely involves direct contact between the media producer and the audience (an exception being the radio phone-in). How can those working in the media 'know' their audience in order to speak to them? Some feedback occurs in the form of letters sent in and so on, but it is doubtful that these are really representative of the audience. Letter writers tend to be more middle class and educated. Surveys of audiences may be conducted, and ratings or circulation figures reflect general levels of popularity. Otherwise, those in the media must make do with an image of their audience, a 'typical' viewer, listener or reader.

Audience position

However, the media do address us, talk to us and weave us into the flow of communication. When we take a photograph or paint a picture we are providing a **point of view** for someone looking at the picture, as in the advert below.

The same can be said of film and television, which have their own ways of positioning the audience. When telling

Figure 6.8

Figure 6.9

a story, TV and film cameras usually construct a point of view. The camera shot creates the viewer's perspective on events. Generally, this is as an onlooker from the outside. The viewer then has the pleasure of knowing more than the characters in a story as the camera will make sense of events for the viewer rather than the subjects. This can be the basis for suspense as we anticipate the outcome. For example, in the film *Psycho*, the camera switches between the 'victim to be', Janet Leigh, who is in the shower, and the approaching attacker with his knife. A more unusual point of view is provided in *Halloween* where the camera represents the view of the killer, so that the victim's look of shock is directed at us, the viewers. In *The Blair Witch Project* the audience shares the horrific experiences of the main characters firsthand, seeing the events via their camcorder recordings. The camera's ability to position audiences like this helps to shape horror movies as a genre.

Audiences may also be positioned in terms of the person they are led to identify with. Through whose eyes are the events viewed? For example, in traditional westerns, the events are typically seen through the eyes of the 'hero' as opposed to the 'villain(s)'.

As explained in Chapter 2, such effects are **naturalized** by means of the various filming conventions – that is, we are not made aware of how it is achieved, rather we simply take it for granted as audiences.

This is rather different in non-fiction television (as discussed in Source 6.8 on TV presenters), where viewers are likely to be acknowledged verbally and visually (by direct address).

ACTIVITY

Record on video a three-minute sequence from a film shown on television. Write a short account, explaining how the camera shots create a point of view.

Source 6.8 TV presenters

1 How do TV presenters help to position the audience for TV programmes?
2 Why are members of the public not allowed to look directly at the camera?
An interesting exercise in breaking TV conventions, for those with access to video cameras, is to conduct an interview where the interviewee answers questions directly into the camera rather than to the interviewer.
3 What effect does the auto-cue create for the presenter?
4 Apart from game and quiz shows, when else do presenters directly address the audience?

Source 6.8 (Jane Root, *Open the Box*, Comedia Methuen, 1986)

" TV presenters

Often, they appear to act as mediators, occupying a curious position half way between the sitting rooms of those watching and the experiences which are being shown on television. Their 'invitations' imply they can help us to enter otherwise obscure worlds. On documentaries they point out things we might miss; on talk shows, they introduce their famous guests to us.

This convention is exaggerated by the presenter's language, especially their use of an inclusive we. The presenter may say 'we are going to talk to x': in reality they mean they are going to have the conversation while we eavesdrop. A similarly bizarre convention lies behind the tag lines of many presenters of light entertainment. It was all very well for Bruce Forsyth to proclaim 'Nice to see you; to see you nice' on The Generation Game but obviously he couldn't see the viewers at all. The same, of course, applies to all those hosts who sign off by saying 'see you next week.'

The most important device in this relationship, however, is that of direct address. Interviewees, especially ordinary members of the public are not usually shown looking directly at the camera. It is only presenters who can regularly 'catch the camera's eye' and stare at the viewers, a strategy which makes those watching feel they are being personally addressed.

The invention of the auto-cue – a machine which reflects the words printed on a roll of paper onto a mirror in front of the camera – helped to strengthen the ritual of direct address. Skilled use of this machine allows the presenter to speak continuously without looking down from the camera to consult notes. The smooth, fluent diction which results tends to give an intense impression of interest and knowledge, even if the presenter is simply parroting words they don't understand.

MODE OF ADDRESS

Apart from positioning us as viewer, reader and so on, the media address us as people – that is, they use ideas of who we are and our relationship to the media as audiences. For example, newspapers use language that is thought appropriate for its readers (see pages 17–18).

Family and nation

The larger the audience, the more difficult it is to define its membership. Cinema's appeal has normally been one of privacy – the individual watching in darkness. In contrast, television (and previously radio) adopts a **domestic** mode of address – it is a family medium. Indeed, television family viewing policy provides four time bands for:

- children;
- family viewing or children alone;
- children viewing with parents' approval;
- no programmes suitable for children.

Broadcasters, especially the BBC, have long addressed the audience in terms of a national 'family'. Indeed, it sees itself as a national institution representing the key events that it considers to be of national interest, including the Queen's speech at Christmas, the State opening of Parliament, the FA Cup Final, royal weddings and so on. Television is the one medium where there can occasionally be a sense of national participation, with audiences of over 25 million being recorded for very popular events, which become a point of everyday conversation the following day.

Source 6.9

Contrast the *Radio Times* and *TV Times* covers in their differing modes of address.

Why do they differ?

ACTIVITIES

1 Examine the BBC and ITV schedules, then identify which programme time bands are aimed at which family members.
2 Compare the modes of address used by presenters to speak to distinctive age groups – children, youth and the retired, for example, – in programmes scheduled at differing times of the day.
3 List the various types of family represented on television, such as in situation comedies, quiz shows and adverts. Which kind of family is most often represented?

79p **11–17 December 1999** www.radiotimes.com

LONDON

RadioTimes

We 'umbly present a sneak preview of the best of festive TV

A Dickens of a
Christmas

Nicholas Lyndhurst stars as Uriah Heep in David Copperfield

18–31 December 1999

RadioTimes

9 770961 887071

5 0 >

Alan Titchmarsh gifts for gardeners **Ross Burden** wines to cheer

Source 6.9b

Sources 6.10 a and b

1 How do these two adverts for sports shoes address different genders?
2 What do they say about masculinity and femininity?

ACTIVITY

Collect 10-12 adverts from magazines you think adopt a masculine or feminine mode of address. Identify the features that distinguish which sex is being addressed.

In high street newsagents there is usually a section of magazines for women. In recent years, there has also been a growth of magazines explicitly aimed at male readers (apart from the traditional 'top shelf' soft porn titles). However, the majority of magazines are only implicitly targeting male or female readers. In other words, the front covers are coded in such a way that they address either a masculine or a feminine audience.

Source 6.10a

Source 6.10b

Source 6.11a

Source 6.11c (*Max*, March 1998)

Source 6.11b (*Practical Photography*, June 1992)

Sources 6.12 a, b, c and d

Which kinds of female audience are being addressed in these magazine covers? Consider:
1 the title;
2 the dominant image (ideal reader?) including age, appearance, body language, how photographed and accompanying anchorage (see page 14);
3 the price;
4 coverlines of promised content;
5 design including typeface, graphics, layout and so on.

Source 6.12b (*Marie Claire*, December 1999)

J-17

THE WORLD'S COOLEST MAG... DEFINITELY

SPLASH DOWN!
20 PAGES OF SUMMER FASHION

WIN! £1,250 IN OUR TALENT COMP

"I look like a girl!"
Adam Rickitt proves he's all boy

Kidnapped!
Parents who have their kids locked up (just for staying out late)

4 ways to fall in love
Which one do you do?

This mag will make famo

How to get a job in TV, music or
Go to fame school The J17 tale

PLUS BRAD RENFRO RYAN PHILLIPPE REESE WITHER
SARAH MICHELLE GELLAR A1 JOE ABSOLOM AND H

Source 6.12a (*J-17*, July 1999)

DECEMBER 1999 £2.50

UK EDITION

marie claire

THE REAL REASON HE DIDN'T CALL

VOYEURDORM: WHERE GIRLS ARE FILMED 24 HOURS A DAY

COCAINE ON THE CATWALK

STRETCH MARKS, BAD SEX, LEAKING BREASTS: THE TRUTH ABOUT HAVING A BABY

Disco inferno
101 ways to dress like a diva

Win £10,000 to shop till you drop
15% off
French Connection Buy Mail

Source 6.12c (*Take a Break*, 11 November 1999)

Source 6.12d (*Pride*, December 1999)

HOW MUCH INFLUENCE?

Millions of people spend several hours of each week watching television, reading newspapers and so on. It is not surprising that many claims have been made about the media's influence on audiences.

The passive audience

Throughout this century, it has been argued that the media have had a strong effect on audiences. Earlier in the century it was believed wartime propaganda and later Nazi propaganda in Germany were examples of this influence. In the 1950s, advertising was seen as persuading people to buy products in ways they did not realize. In these ways the power of the media has been likened to a '**hypodermic needle**'. Great concern has been voiced about the possible harmful effects of the media on young people. When this builds up to a great intensity – often via the popular press – the situation is referred to as a **moral panic**. A range of voices of authority – MPs, Church leaders, police chiefs – demand that action be taken to control the cause of the problem. In the past, cinema, pop music, radio and television have all at times been blamed for social problems concerning young people, especially violent behaviour. The most recent moral panics have been about videos, video games and the Internet.

The media and violence: research problems

The method

Much of the research investigating whether or not violence in the media causes more violence generally involves setting up experiments, where young people are shown a diet of violent programmes and then interviewed and/or observed to see how they have been affected. What might be the problems of this approach?

Figure 6.10 (*The Times*, 13 April 1994)

The essence of a video is that it is shown in the home and I'm afraid you know people who say that 'why shouldn't adults be able to see this kind of thing in their own home?' I'm half tempted to say that people who make that kind of demand knowing that children are likely to see it, aren't really themselves very mature and adult. There are places where people can go and see this material if they want it but we're talking about material in the home and there has now been tragic story after tragic story of the effect of this type of material on the children.

Mary Whitehouse (President, National Viewers' and Listeners' Association)

Source 6.13 (*Open Space*, BBC 2, 14 June 1984)

Source 6.13 Video nasties

What kind of effect on children do you think Mary Whitehouse is referring to in connection with watching videos?

Figure 6.11 (*The Express*, 8 May 1999)

Violence

What kind of effect?

Researchers cannot agree on how audiences are affected regarding violence. Among the effects suggested are the following.

- **Imitation,** meaning that some people will be encouraged to copy the type of behaviour shown (as suggested by *The Daily Telegraph* article in Figure 6.12).
- **Catharsis,** meaning that, by experiencing the violence second-hand, audiences will be able to release their own aggression and frustration, and thereby become more relaxed and non-violent.
- **Desensitization,** meaning that being exposed to a steady stream of violent images causes audiences to become numb and accepting rather than shocked or concerned.

The biggest criticism of the 'hypodermic needle' argument is that it does not fully take into account how active the audience is in receiving the media.

> *Dr Belson in his much discussed 'effects' book, Television Violence and the Adolescent Boy, gives a classification of the 'Violence Rating' of a whole series of programmes. Yogi Bear gets a rating of 1.42, Steptoe and Son 2.39, Hawaii Five-O 7.25, and The Great War 7.62. Incredible as it may sound, they assumed that the BBC's series on the mass slaughter of World War I affected audiences in the same way as a light-hearted cop series. According to Belson, both play a part in inciting teenagers to delinquency and both should be censored.*

Source 6.14 (J. Root, *Open the Box*, Comedia/Methuen, 1986)

Figure 6.12 (*The Daily Telegraph*, 1 April 1994)

Catalogue of cruelty: rental shop shelves crammed with the type of potentially harmful videos that more than 200 MPs want to ban

Suspected link with crime cited in three murder trials

Video linked to Bulger case

VIDEO nasties have been linked specifically to acts of torture and violence and cited as a general reason for antisocial behaviour among children.

Videos such as *Child's Play*, a sadistic horror film, and *Juice*, about gang warfare, have been referred to in recent murder cases.

Following the James Bulger case in November, it was noted that Mr Jon Venables, father of one of James's killers, had hired a video of the film *Child's Play 3*.

The film depicts a doll which turns into a child and is subsequently killed by two boys on a ghost train. An 18 certificate film directed by Jack Bender, it features a doll called Chucky which is

By Dan Conaghan

possessed by an evil killer and dressed in toddler's clothing.

Violence enacted on a railway line and use of blue paint was echoed in James's murder.

Mr Justice Morland, who presided over the trial at Preston Crown Court, said that while it was not for him to pass judgment on the children's upbringing, he suspected "exposure to violent video films may in part be an explanation".

In December, three members of a gang who tortured 16-year-old Suzanne Capper for a week before burning her alive were jailed for life after a judge at Manchester

Crown Court described their crime as being "as appalling a murder as it was possible to imagine".

One of the culprits often imagined herself to be a demonic doll featured in *Child's Play*, a video horror film in the same series.

Before inflicting each new round of sadistic violence, she would chant the film's menacing catchphrase: "I'm Chucky. Wanna play?"

Earlier this month, four men were convicted of killing Les Reed, 46, who had remonstrated with them for vandalising traffic bollards in Cardiff. Some of those who repeatedly kicked and stamped Mr Reed had previously watched a video of the film *Juice*, in which a shop-

keeper is murdered for trying to enforce law and order.

One was said to have repeated a line from the film — "I have got the juice" — following the murder. The film title is American slang for "respect".

The active audience

Doubts about how easily audiences are influenced by the media were raised by American researchers in the 1940s and 1950s. Their work showed that audience members used 'defence' mechanisms to resist media messages. These might include **selective exposure**, which would include only reading a newspaper that voices political opinions you agree with; and **selective perception**, which is interpreting what you see so that it is consistent with your current attitudes and beliefs.

Further 'protection' from the media was also found to come from the social groups to which audiences belong. As a result of this research, the original question, 'What does the media do to people?' was reversed to 'What do people do with the media?'

This question has been particularly pursued by semiologists (see pages 12-15), who see media products as texts that may be read (or **decoded**) in many different ways. The wider the range of possible meanings of any text, the more it is **polysemic**. Using the example of violence, it is doubtful that audiences share the same interpretations of which films or television programmes could be seen as promoting or encouraging violence. As another example, look at the case study on Lara Croft in Chapter 1.

Source 6.15 (RAJAR, *Insight* 1999)

AUDIENCE RECEPTION

What shapes our reception of the media?

Uses and gratifications

This is based on the belief that audiences have certain needs (or uses) that they seek to satisfy (or gratify) in the media. The main four categories singled out are:

1 **diversion** – escape or emotional release (forgetting everyday worries);
2 **personal relationships** – companionship or as topic for discussion ('Did you see ...?');
3 **personal identity** – making comparison with your own situation ('Do they have the same problem?');
4 **surveillance** – seeking information about the world ('What is going on?').

The nature of radio relationships

There are two key facets to listeners' requirements from radio - the first is a functional requirement, while the second is an emotional one.

The functional requirement is the need for information - news, time checks, traffic news, weather or sports results. This was well demonstrated by the respondent who described how listening to the radio could make the difference between her journey to work taking 30 minutes or an hour and a half.

The emotional requirement is characterized by listeners in terms of the relationship they have with either a presenter or a particular music show – 'Chris Tarrant gets us in the right mood for the day ahead', 'I tune to Kiss FM each night to keep in touch with the club scene'.

Breakfast
At breakfast time, the functional element is at its highest. The most successful breakfast DJs are seen by listeners as those that are able to fulfil their functional role as a provider of news, travel, weather etc., while at the same time providing an emotional feel-good factor – it's not surprising that virtually all radio stations' programming reflects this functional requirement in the morning.

The choice of station is likely to be the same day after day and is probably the one that the radio alarm clock is tuned to.

Daytime
During the daytime, radio is used in a classic background mode and this is seen as a positive attribute by listeners. The relationship is uncritical and undemanding, with the result that the medium is used to create the right atmosphere to accompany daytime tasks.

In this role, the presenter is very important, with listeners seeking out programmes on the basis of who the presenter is. Listeners are looking for the character to come from the presenter – maybe they have the right tone of voice or a particular sense of humour – and they actively seek out particular programmes during the daytime.

Listeners outside of the office make personal choices of stations from across their repertoire. In contrast, listening in the workplace relies on consensus and leads to more habitual station choice.

An interviewee who listened in the office summed up the role of radio during the day - 'the radio keeps the mood just right'.

Evening/weekends
It is during the evening and at weekends that listeners are most likely to seek out particular music shows by appointment. Radio station programming again reflects this need, with the scheduling of specialist music shows at these times - Kiss FM specializes in different strands of dance music each evening, while other examples include Dinner Jazz and Radio 1's Essential Selection.

ACTIVITY

Compare your own use of radio with that described in Source 6.15. Which part of your listening is 'functional' and which 'emotional'? Is it always possible to separate your listening into these two categories?

Source 6.16 Researching uses and gratifications

ACTIVITY

Source 6.16 is a uses and gratifications survey for detective/crime TV series. It can be applied to any media. To conduct your own survey, you need to do the following.

1 Obtain a list of possible reasons for watching a particular programme or genre (soap opera or game show, say) by asking a sample of people to say why they enjoy watching such programmes.
2 Try to group together similar answers under one statement. For example, 'I like watching soap opera because we discuss it at home' and 'I talk to my mates about it' could be 'I like talking to others about it'.
3 Supply your list to a group to complete as in the example to the right. Who you ask will depend on what kind of audience you want to research – it may include a mixture of age groups, sexes or social classes (usually based on occupation – see Figure 6.6).

Levels of attention

The problem with the uses and gratification approach is that it assumes media usage is carefully selected by individual members of an audience.

Recent research into audiences suggests that people's attention to different media varies considerably. To reflect this, distinctions between primary, secondary and tertiary media activities have been made. Primary activity means giving the media close attention. Secondary activity means there may be other distractions, such as talking to someone else, and tertiary means that the media is just in the background. Obviously this division is not precise, but it does recognize different levels of attention.

Much depends on the medium in question and the conditions in which it is received. Cinema is nearly always a primary activity. The dark surroundings, large image and admission fee all contribute to the audience being closely involved with the film.

In comparison, radio is often a secondary or tertiary medium, as when it is simply on in the background and the person is doing something else, such as working in an office or shopping. Having said that, the fact that radio is a very mobile medium means it can be received in quite intimate or private situations, such as in bed or while driving a car.

This is part of a study of reasons for enjoying detective/crime series on television. Will you please indicate how strongly you agree or disagree with each of the following statements, by placing a tick in the appropriate column. (1 strongly agree, 2 agree, 3 neutral, 4 disagree, 5 strongly disagree.)

Reason for watching	1	2	3	4	5
I like to identify with the hero.					
I like to talk about the shows with others.					
I like the tension of not knowing what is going to happen.					
It makes me aware of how difficult a job the police have.					
I like to imagine how I would cope with a violent situation.					

Note: It is usually necessary to collect some data about the respondent (sex, age, occupation, educational level).

Source 6.16 (John Fiske, *Introduction to Communication Studies,* Methuen, 1982)

Figure 6.13 Primary or secondary activity?

It seems that television, too, is often a secondary medium. Indeed, in some homes, it is kept on continuously, regardless of whether or not anyone is watching. This has been shown by the results of an interesting experiment when a small video camera was placed inside viewers' TV sets, so that they could be watched while watching TV! The extract (Source 6.18) describes some of the findings of this experiment.

Activities and use of radio and television between 7.30 and 7.45 on weekday mornings, summer, 1983			
	Total (%)	Men (%)	Women (%)
Eating/drinking	16	15	17
Washing/dressing	13	7	15
Preparing food/washing up	10	6	18
At work/school	8	14	5
Talking/phoning	7	5	8
Travelling to work/school	7	7	3
Housework	6	3	12
Care of children	5	2	11
Reading/writing	4	5	3
Care of pets	2	1	2
Hobbies & games	1	1	0
Gardening	1	1	0
Relaxing	1	2	1
Listening to radio	23	21	29

Source 6.17 (Nadine Dyer, *BBC Audience Research Findings*, 1986)

> *The evidence of the videotapes shows that people have their eyes on the screen only about 65 per cent of the time that they are in the room. For the rest of the time they attend to the kids, groom themselves, read the newspaper or doze off – the list of distractions is endless. The tapes also show that even when people have their eyes glued to the screen, they frequently engage in activities that have nothing to do with television-watching. A high proportion of these activities, like ironing, knitting, sewing and talking on the telephone while watching TV, are performed by women. This could be due to the sense of guilt that women report about watching television, but it may also be related to the fact that they have more domestic work to do.*
>
> *One of the striking things to emerge from the tapes is the frequency with which people's viewing patterns are influenced by the choice and actions of others. Ever since media researchers first turned their attention to television, they have happily assumed that the best way to study television is to look at individual viewers – at the programmes they enjoy, how much they remember, and the effect that television has on them. Because television research has concentrated on the experiences of individuals, it has overlooked the essentially social nature of a good deal of television watching. Even today, with the number of multi-set homes and VCRs growing, it remains the case that a fair amount of viewing takes place when more than one person is in the room. Under these circumstances, it frequently happens that family members want to watch different programmes, or that one person wants to watch television while another wants to do something that conflicts with TV viewing. The video material is full of such instances – cases, for example, where the man wants to watch Match of the Day and his wife wants to watch a feature film, or where the children want a bedtime story and the parents remain determined to watch the news.*
>
> *Conflicts of interest over the television often lead to family disputes, to bouts of sulking and, more frequently than one imagines, to physical tussles over the remote control. The remote control has become the latest symbol of power. Parents will go to extreme lengths to withhold it from their children, and children will use all kinds of tricks to keep it away from their siblings. We have even recorded one case where the father gets up to make a cup of coffee for his wife and takes the remote control to the kitchen with him.*

Source 6.18 (Peter Collett, *The Listener*, 22 May 1986)

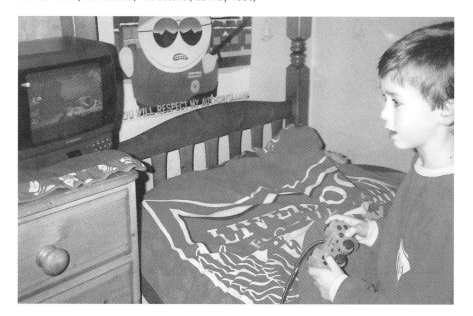

The rise of bedroom culture

Until quite recently it was the norm for families to gather around the television (and prior to television, the radio set) in the living room. However, it seems that this collective viewing is in decline. The 1999 *Young People New Media* Report (by Sonia Livingston and Moira Bovill) reveals how children (aged 6–17) are increasingly developing a 'bedroom culture' that involves spending a significant amount of time watching TV, playing computer games, using the Internet and listening to music. This trend has developed as a result of children acquiring more and more media technology for their bedrooms (see page 6), and spending less time outdoors (partly due to parental fears for children's safety).

This 'bedroom culture' allows children to create a private world with limited parental control. The research confirms that it is at 'bedtime' that children are most likely to enter into this private culture where they might stay up watching TV (past the 9.00 watershed hour), send and receive e-mails, join in Internet 'chat boxes', and other media related activities. Whilst acknowledging there might be the occasional computer or television 'addict', the authors of *Young People New Media* are positive about what they see as the essentially social nature of this 'bedroom culture'. They claim it helps children build up their own identity and forms a strong point of reference within friendship groups, whether that be gossiping about TV characters, sharing the latest computer games or chatting online.

Figure 6.14

Gender and reception

One aspect that the research has raised is how males and females differ in their reception of the media. One researcher, David Morley, has found that men are more likely to plan their television viewing in advance than women – by checking the television listings, for example. Furthermore, the men have a clear preference for viewing silently without interruption so as not to miss anything, while women tend to think of TV as a social activity, perhaps carrying on conversations while viewing. Another difference includes preferred programmes, with male viewers opting more for sport and women for soap opera. Some potential reasons for this are offered in the comments made to Dorothy Hobson (DH) in her interviews with female viewers of *Crossroads* which was a popular soap opera in the 1970s–1980s.

> **Source 6.19** *Crossroads* and its audience
>
> 1 List the main reasons for *Crossroads'* appeal to female viewers.
> 2 Why, then, do you think soap operas have more appeal for women than men?

As described in Source 6.18, women are often unable to give full attention to the media because of domestic tasks, such as cleaning, cooking or child minding. Even so, there are occasions when women are able to watch television, read magazines, listen to the radio and so on without distractions or resistance from others. This most typically occurs when they are at home during the day. It is not unusual for groups of women to view hired videos, one popular form being the long family saga covering two or three tapes.

(DH = Dorothy Hobson, who is the interviewer in these discussions)

DH I wonder when men criticize it and say it's rubbish and all that. I mean, it occurs to me that if it was such rubbish then why do they make such a fuss about women watching it?

J They don't like it 'cos it's sometimes sentimental.

DH And you think women like it for that reason?

J Yes, because men are not supposed to show their emotions and feelings and so if they watch *Crossroads* and something comes on like Glenda and Kath talking, then they think it's just stupid and unrealistic because they are not brought up to accept emotional situations.

DH So you think it is more a programme that women like?

J Yes, it is, I think. I don't know any men who watch it.

DH I know some but certainly not many. But not only do they – I mean not watch it, but some of them are really quite hostile to their wives watching it.

DH Why do you like *Crossroads*?

A Just that you like to know what's going to happen next, you know. I mean they're terrible actors, I know that, and I just see through that, you know. I just, now and then I think, 'Oh my God, that's silly', you know, but it's not the acting I'm interested in, it's what's going on. I suppose I'm nosey...

J Well, it's easy to watch. It's not relaxing but it's not something that's, like, tense. I mean, you follow the stories but you are not sort of keyed up about it. It's sort of teatime viewing but not in the sense that you would usually use tea time viewing, do you know what I mean?

DH What do you mean when you say, 'Not in the sense that you would normally use teatime viewing'? How would you normally use it then?

J Well people have got to stop and watch *Crossroads* 'cos it's on at teatime but with other things you are like rushing around getting the tea and talking and it's sort of in the background.

DH So you would never have it on in the background? You would always stop and watch it?

J No, you couldn't follow it.

M I like family stories and things like that. I like something with a story.

DH So you think that's the reason that you like it?

M Yes, because it continues, and personally I think it's a lot like real life.

DH In what way?

M Well, I mean Jill had her ups and downs, didn't she, and so did Meg, and whatsit with her kiddie who she wants from America, I mean that can happen in real life, can't it? To me it's things in there that can happen in real life. It's not fiction to me. To me it's a real family story.

Source 6.19 (Dorothy Hobson, *Crossroads, the Drama of a Soap Opera*, Methuen, 1982)

How might the gender-based television choices shown be explained?

Source 6.20 (ITC, *Television: The Public View*, 1998)

GENDER AND TELEVISION PREFERENCES	
Female bias	**Male bias**
Most interest	*Most interest*
Soap operas	Sports
Plays and drama	Sitcoms
Health and medical	Alternative comedy
Hobbies and leisure	Adult-only films
Quiz/panel games	Science
Chat shows	Current affairs
Variety shows	Pop and rock music
Consumer affairs	Europe
Children's programmes	Business and finance
Religion	Politics
Least interest	*Least interest*

SEX EXCLUSIVITY FOR TOP 40 PROGRAMMES BY TV RATINGS 1998	
Programmes featuring in the men's top 40 but not the women's.	Programmes featuring in the women's top 40 but not the men's.
World Cup matches:	*Emmerdale*
France v. Croatia and	*Diana: Crash secrets*
12 other matches	*Birds of a Feather*
They Think It's All Over	*Coronation Street*
Champions League Football	*Coming Home*
Police, Camera, Action	*Dinner Ladies*
Grand National	*Where the Heart Is*
Die Hard (film)	*Airline*
Harry Enfield	*Nannies from Hell*
March in Windy City	*Real Women*
	Peak Practice
	Men for Sale

Source 6.21 (Taris, *UK Television and Video Yearbook*, 1999)

AUDIENCE ACCESS

The influence of the audience may be felt by whether or not people buy the newspapers, watch the television programmes, go to see the films and so on. This, however, is only a crude reflection of audience reactions to what is produced. How far can viewers, listeners and readers directly communicate their feelings to media producers?

ACTIVITY

List all the ways you can think of contacting television/radio broadcasters and newspaper/magazine publishers to give your views about what they produce.

Individuals may not be able to have much influence on their own. By joining an organized group, however, you may be taken more seriously. Apart from groups of the likes of political parties and trade unions, there are some organizations set up solely to influence the media.

Sources 6.22 a and b Media pressure groups

1 What seem to be the aims of each of these organizations?
2 Who do you think has most power in the relationship between media producers and the audience? Give reasons for your answers.

Introducing the NATIONAL VIEWERS' AND LISTENERS' ASSOCIATION

All Saints' House, High Street, COLCHESTER, CO1 1UG. Tel: 01206 561155

Mrs Mary Whitehouse CBE
Founder & President Emeritus

The Association was founded in 1964 by Mary Whitehouse CBE, and her associates, because as a teacher she was finding that television was attacking and undermining the very fabric of Christian civilisation. Speaking in 1964, at the Birmingham Town Hall, she said *"If violence is shown as normal on the television screen, it will help to create violent society"*.

What do we believe?

The National Viewers' and Listeners' Association believes that:

- violence on television contributes significantly to the increase of violence in society and should be curtailed in the public interest.
- the use of swearing and blasphemy are destructive of our culture and our Christian faith; also that the broadcasting authorities are failing to meet their legal obligations by allowing the frequent use of offensive language.
- sexual innuendo and explicit sex trivialise and cheapen human relationships whilst undermining marriage and family life.
- the media are indivisible and that broadcasting standards are inevitably affected by the standards of film, theatre and publishing.

What do we aim to achieve?

The National Viewers' and Listeners' Association aims to:

- encourage viewers and listeners to react effectively to programme content - for example in writing, by telephoning and by writing letters to the press.
- initiate and stimulate public discussion and parliamentary debate concerning the effects of broadcasting, and other mass media, on the individual, the family and society.
- secure - and then uphold - effective legislation to control obscenity and pornography in the media, including Broadcasting, from Britain and abroad.

Source 6.22a

CAMPAIGN FOR PRESS AND BROADCASTING FREEDOM

The **Campaign for Press and Broadcasting Freedom** was launched in 1979 to campaign for diverse, democratic and accountable media. It has the support of 26 national trade unions and numerous union branches, Constituency Labour Parties and individual members. We are the nation's leading pressure group working for a genuinely **free** and **democratic** media.

Our objectives include:

• To challenge the myths of 'impartiality' and 'balance' in broadcasting and 'objectivity' in newspapers by campaigning for the genuine presentation of the **diversity** and **plurality** of society.

• To challenge the myth that only private ownership of the newspaper industry provides genuine **freedom, diversity** or **access.**

• To challenge the myth that the present forms of ownership and regulation of broadcasting guarantee editorial **independence,** democratic **accountability** or **high programme standards.**

• To carry out research and generate debate on **alternative** forms of ownership and control of the media industries, and to encourage **alternative forms** of media control.

• To work for press and broadcasting that are free of materials that are **detrimental** to any individual or group on the grounds of gender, race, class, religion, sexual preference, age or physical or mental ability.

• To encourage debate on the **implications** of technological advances in the media, to ensure that the **public interest** is **safe-guarded** and that commercial interests do not override **public accountability.**

• To campaign for the replacement of the Press Complaints Commission and the Broadcasting Complaints Commission with a statutory based Media Commission with the power to enforce the **Right To Reply.**

AIMS

In other chapters of this book the emphasis has been on developing an understanding of key concepts relating to media studies via practical exercises. Only by means of firsthand experience is it possible to properly understand how something 'works'. The creative process of producing a media text provides insights that are unlikely to be as effective as merely reading about or discussing the process.

Indeed, for many students the attraction of media studies is the opportunity to participate, however remotely, in the excitement and glamour that are widely perceived to be part of media production. However, it is important to be aware of the disappointments that are likely to arise if this is the main motivation for pursuing a media course. First, the goal of media studies is to *understand* the media, not become a television producer, journalist or whatever. Knowledge of production techniques in itself is not enough. There needs to be an awareness of how and why particular techniques work, what effect they might have and so on.

Furthermore, it is unlikely a school or college will have the resources needed to achieve the high technical standards that typify professional media production. That is not to say it is impossible or undesirable to produce high-quality media work with relatively low-cost equipment, but merely to try and copy what is seen as 'proper' media production is likely to lead to disappointment and inhibit the broader aim of *reflection*. This means thinking about what has been learned during the process of media production work.

Above all, production work should be seen as a means of illuminating understanding of the key themes and concepts that are the focus of other chapters in this book. This means reflecting on the following themes and questions.

- *Forms and language*
  How do media texts create meaning?
- *Representations*
  What ideas about the world are contained in media texts?
- *Audiences*
  How do audiences respond to, and make sense of, media texts?
- *Institutions*
  How is media production influenced by wider factors, such as finances, technology and regulation?

Figure 7.1

THE PRODUCTION PROCESS

Individual or group work

While there are benefits in working individually on media productions – not having to consult or negotiate, setting your own deadlines and so on – most production work in media industries is collective in nature. This is because few individuals have the diverse range of skills that are usually needed. These might include writing/scripting, designing, performing/presenting, editing and so on, as well as any specialist technical skills required to use the technology effectively.

If you choose to work primarily as an individual, then it is probably a good idea to enlist other people's support. For example, as a magazine 'editor' you might commission others to write features or provide artwork. As a radio producer, you might prefer someone whose voice is better suited to radio than your own to be on air. Video production work is very difficult without a team, so again additional help might be required to operate cameras, appear as a presenter and so on. The key point is that as an individual you have responsibility for the main ideas that shape the overall production.

When you work with others as a group, it is important to decide on an appropriate division of labour based on who seems best suited to each role. Alternatively, you might like to rotate the roles so that everyone has some experience of each aspect of production and is able to make an approximately equal contribution to the end product. Group work requires a strong willingness to cooperate and share. No one individual should be indispensable and there should be some inbuilt plan to deal with cases of anyone failing to deliver what they have promised.

Part or whole production

There is a lot of satisfaction to be gained from completing a 'whole' production that can be presented as such to an audience, whether it be a video documentary, magazine or other project. However, in practical terms, the limitations of time and technology are such that it is often not possible to undertake such 'complete' or 'whole' productions. Furthermore, the biggest danger for students thinking about media production work is being overambitious. In attempting to create something on a scale that needs considerable resources (not least that of time), there is almost an inevitable loss of quality and control that leads to sloppy or rushed work.

It is much more sensible to attempt to produce something that is manageable enough to ensure both good-quality standards of execution and an adequate understanding of the relevant medium or genre that is involved. For example, in print media, producing the front cover of a magazine and/or a double-page feature is sufficiently challenging as a production task; rather than attempting to produce a complete magazine of 16–24 pages. Likewise, a ten-minute radio feature or 'package' is ample as an exercise in demonstrating a grasp of radio codes and conventions, whereas attempting a 30-minute-long programme would be foolhardy.

What to produce

Choosing a subject

There is no point in spending hours on producing something in which you have little or no interest. For a start, it is unlikely that you will have sufficient knowledge to tackle the subject effectively, and, second, the lack of interest will show through in the end product. You need to identify a topic or area in which you have an interest and already have some expertise, or at least are keen to learn more. However, it should also be a subject that has some appeal to a wider audience than yourself and your immediate friends!

The target audience

Media production without a well-defined audience is likely to lack a clear sense of purpose. The choice of language, look or style for any media product implies who is likely to be its target audience. The main categories to consider in defining your audience include:

- **age** 14–16 or 17–21 and so on;
- **gender** male, female or non-gender-specific;
- **lifestyle** family, single and so on;
- **income/education**;
- **specialist knowledge**.

The right medium

Not every subject is suited to all media forms. For example, snooker does not easily lend itself to radio coverage! On the other hand, it is difficult to make talk and discussion interesting on video. In judging which media form would be best for your subject, consideration should be given to the importance of:

- **visuals** – moving images, settings, action are suited to **video**;
- **sound** – speech, music are suited to **radio**;
- **detail** – facts, narrative, need for future reference are suited to **print**;
- **interactivity** – selection, exploration, feedback are suited to **websites**.

Furthermore, what will be the best way to reach your target audience? Are they more likely to respond to a particular medium because of their own pattern of media usage? Is the audience likely to respond at a primary or secondary level of attention? (see pages 135–6).

(see pages 135–6).

ACTIVITY

For each of the following subjects, select what you think would be the most and least effective choices of media form, giving reasons for your choices.

- fashion feature;
- profile of a pop band;
- football club news and match reports;
- a student holiday diary.

STAGES OF PRODUCTION

Pre-production

Research

Before starting any practical work, it is essential that there is adequate planning and preparation. The first requirement is to undertake research. This can be based on a number of needs, as follows.

- *Comparable media products*
  What are the common codes and conventions used? How is the audience addressed? What works well and could be successfully adapted for your production?
- *The subject*
  Do you have all the necessary information regarding your chosen subject? Are there additional materials (such as images) that you need to gather?

Planning

This involves making detailed plans for the production work, including scripts, storyboards, draft page designs, mock-ups and a clear outline of responsibilities and deadlines. The most frequent problem identified by students reflecting on their production experience is the failure to plan properly and set realistic deadlines, which has led to serious difficulties with time management.

The golden rule? *You should always build in more time than you think you will need.* In the unlikely event of your finishing ahead of schedule, you can spend extra time on the critical account – an important part of the process.

(Of course, this only applies to hands-on production work. It may be that the exercise is purely a planning assignment rather than a completed practical production.)

Production

This involves the actual application of technology to make your media product. This could be video cameras, radio equipment, desktop publishing or other equipment. Hopefully, you will already have had an opportunity to become familiar with how it works. Otherwise, a significant amount of time might be used up discovering how to do things by trial and error before you are confident in using the equipment.

It is normal to encounter technical problems – equipment breaks down, batteries run out, computers crash and so on. Time for this should be allowed in your planning. Ideally specialist technical assistance is available. However, it should always be remembered that *judgements made about the quality of media production work should take into account the nature of the technology available to students.*

Figure 7.2

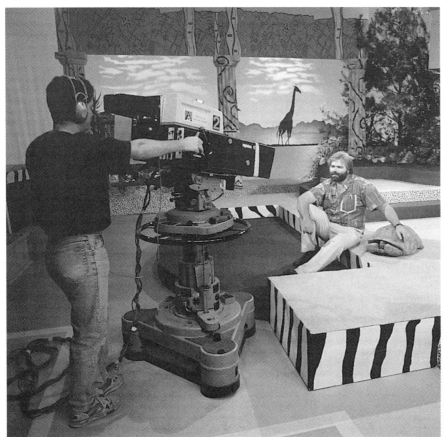

Broadcast-standard films are not expected using a domestic camcorder with only an internal microphone!

Post-production

What is generally meant by this term is the work undertaken to ensure that the 'raw material' recorded on audio and videotape is edited to create a smooth flow. This can be very time-consuming depending on how close the recordings are to the intended end product. Increasingly, digital editing (using computer software) is replacing traditional analogue editing, such as VHS editing suites or reel-to-reel tape recorders.

In the case of print media, there is a need to 'package' your material effectively. This could mean using high-quality glossy paper or heat binding of pages to achieve a more professional finish.

Figure 7.3

The critical account

All production work needs to include a written account, which discusses the following.

- *The aims of the production*
  What was the purpose of the production? Who was the target audience?
- *Preparation and research*
  What was learned from examining comparable products? What planning went into the production?
- *The production process*
  What were the main ideas that shaped each stage of the production? What problems were encountered and how were they overcome?
- *Critical evaluation*
  What were the main strengths and weaknesses of the production? What insights and understanding about media production have emerged?

In order to write such an account, it is vital to keep some kind of diary or log to record the process by which the production developed. Try to go beyond simply describing what happened and provide *analysis* – the ideas and understanding involved in the experience.

To assess a production's strengths and weaknesses adequately, it is vital to get **audience feedback**. Choose a small sample of your target audience (but ideally not your friends or family as they will be reluctant to be critical). Present your production in conditions that allow you to record their responses. Pose some questions to enable you to identify the most and least effective aspects of the production. Options for recording responses including tape recording (especially if it is a group response) making notes or using a questionnaire. Emphasize the need for the audience to be honest in its responses, so that you can properly assess which parts of the production have been least and most successful and why.

Finally consideration should be given to factors beyond the immediate production issues of design, technology, editing and so on that may have influenced the production process.

These include the following:

- **copyright**
  the need to secure permission in the event of using published material, such as pictures or music;
- **regulation**
  the need to avoid using unacceptable language, inaccuracy or misrepresentation;
- **access**
  to interview people, film in public or private places and so on;
- **distribution**
  how the production may be made available to the target audience.

These are all examples of *institutional factors* that help to shape the outcomes of media production.

Advantages

Radio has a number of features that make it an attractive medium for production work despite its relatively unglamorous image. The technology is cheap and quite simple to use. Basic audio cassette or mini-disc recorders may be used for both recording and editing, although a mixer does offer the significant benefit of multitrack recording.

It is possible to be more ambitious with radio because the technology is more straightforward and the end product enables the audience to use its imagination in 'picturing' the scene. Furthermore, radio is flexible – the equipment is easy to move around, and there is more scope for spontaneity or improvization during the recording. Radio is often exciting because of the generally live nature of the medium (most professional radio output is live).

Considerations

In producing radio material consideration needs to be given to:

- **context**
  the audience needs to be clear about who is talking, the setting and so on;
- **clarity**
  voices on radio need to be easily understood, speech delivered at a reasonable pace and not be too 'quirky', such as having a very strong accent;
- **variety of sound**
  a single presenter or too much pure speech, for example, can easily become monotonous;
- **scripts**
  a carefully prepared script is essential – only the most confident and experienced presenter can rely on improvization alone.

Production ideas

- **Vox pop**
  Vox pop is the name given to an edited sequence of interviews with 'ordinary' people to record instant responses to questions on a particular topic. The aim is to present a sample of public opinion (although much depends on where and when the interviews are recorded).
- **Discussion**
  This is a studio-based debate between people with different points of view, possibly including 'experts'. A chairperson (usually the presenter) leads the discussion. There could be a phone-in element – either using prerecorded questions or comments (taped on an answering machine for the right effect) or via mobile phone links in the studio.
- **A feature (or 'package')**
  A short (5–10-minute) presentation is given on a subject, during which the presenter outlines the key facts and issues using interviews, sound effects and any source that helps to tell the story in a balanced way. It is equivalent to the newspaper or magazine background feature story.

Figure 7.4

Radio assignment

"Here are a few tips and techniques that have helped me. I hope you find them useful."

TONY HERTZ

1 Do a storyboard. I'm not kidding. "Pictures in sound" has become a tired cliché because people worry about the sound and forget the pictures.

If you know what your commercial looks like, you'll find the sounds come a lot easier.

2 Write a two-sentence description of everyone in the commercial, including the end voiceover.

Give them names; flesh them out a bit.

A dialogue featuring MVO1 talking to MVO2 doesn't give actors anything to hang a performance on, which means it won't give the listener much either.

3 Simple is always better. If you've got a good message, try not getting in its way; there's something really exciting about a beautifully-crafted and presented straight commercial.

But if you do write a two-hander, ask yourself the next question:

4 Is it really dialogue? A monologue divided into two parts isn't.

Make sure there's a relationship between your characters, and a reason for the conversation.

This isn't as obvious as it looks.

5 Do your own people-watching. Sitcoms are someone else's observations of real life so if you use television dialogue as a source, you're a generation removed from the original before you start.

Well-executed pastiche is valid. Well-observed life is special.

6 Take your time.

Here's a foolproof method for determining how long a commercial should be:
a) Write it.
b) Read it aloud.
c) Number of seconds taken for step b equals length of commercial.

Any media man, account exec. or client who tells you a radio spot must be any particular length is talking rubbish.

7 Write in a 'bumper' – a line or bit of atmosphere that helps the listener separate your ad from the rubbish that's likely to precede it. Do the same at the end.

8 Take your time (2). Good radio needs as much thinking time as good TV and press, more if you're not used to it. It's worth fighting for.

9 Talk to a specialist about production. (You didn't think you were going to get away without a pitch, did you?)

A good radio director can help even your simple commercials in the same way as a film, type, art or music director.

The closer and earlier you involve him (or her) the better your chance of making it special.

There are maybe half a dozen decent radio production companies – listen to our reels, talk with the directors, go with whoever feels and sounds right.

There are a lot more hints and notes and not enough space, so I may do another ad like this.

Frankly it depends on the reaction to this one.

If you'd like to hear the reel or have a chat, no obligation, call 01-405 0127. Speak to Tony Hertz or Sheila Britten.

THE RADIO OPERATORS, 40 GRAYS INN ROAD, LONDON, WC1X 8LR

Figure 7.5 (*The Complete Guide to Advertising*)

Channel 4 (Boyz Unlimited)

(Musical intro)

DJ/MVO: *Hi, I'm Mike Prince and I'm joined now by the latest boy band sensation Boyz Unlimited. They've got their very own TV show starting this week. Good evening lads.*

    'Hiya'

    'Hi'

So do you want to introduce yourselves?

    'Hi I'm Scott'

    'I'm Jason'

    'I'm Nicky, peace!'

    'I'm Gareth, peace, respect, safe, check it out!'

Well done.

    'And I'm Nigel. I'm the manager and I'm here to make sure you mention the show, you got it?'

Ooh scary man.

    '"Boyz Unlimited", Friday nights 9.30 on Channel 4'

Right eh now let's hear a little bit of your current single. I love it, I've been playing it for weeks and it's called "Stranger Every Day".

    '"Stronger Every Day"'

Yeah whatever.

(Music: Stronger Every Day)

Now I'm here with Boyz Unlimited.

    Sing: 'Hello, Hello, Hello, Hello, Hello'

    'Sorry I've got the flu'

Yeah, nearly worked never mind. So tell us about the TV show.

    'The TV show's called Boyz Unlimited and it starts on Friday nights at 9.30, got it?'

    'We got that Gareth'

    'Is that right after Friends?'

    'That's right'

So what's the show about lads?

    'Well it's a six-part series that follows us around for a whole year'

    'Friday nights, Channel 4, after "Friends"'

    'It just shows some of the crazy things we get up to'

Argh right brilliant, like what?

    'Oh, you know, crazy stuff. We're mad'

    'Oh mad'

Okay, give us an example of how mad you are.

    'Well mate, there was this one time when we tied Scott's shoelaces together'

    'That was so funny'

    'He fell over and fractured his jaw. You should have seen the look on his face'

    'He had to have major reconstructive surgery, it was hilarious. Honestly we're mad'

Now I know you're going to reveal your new single exclusively on the show tonight, so drum roll please.

(SFX: drum roll. Music)

    'It's a cover of an old song you may not have heard of'

    'It's called *A Little Bit More*'

A 'Little Bit More'?

    'That's right'

But you know that um …

    'Are you gonna play this song 'coz you're really starting to annoy me'

Oaky doaky

(Music: A Little Bit More)

Boyz Unlimited there with 'A Little Bit More'.

    'Well what do you reckon then?'

Well you do know that someone has already done that same song?

    'So, we'll release ours first'

Well, they've already released it.

    'No one's gonna remember it are they?'

It was Number One.

    'Oh, right'

    'Sorry, we never listen to the charts … er except the Pepsi Chart Show which we never miss'

Course you don't, course you don't. Right boys thanks for being here today. Do you have a final message for all your fans out there in Fanland?

    'Yeah, "Boyz Unlimited", a new comedy series for Friday nights. Starts the 5th of February 9.30 on Channel 4. Just watch it sunshine'

Yeah I will. Look don't do that with the mikes.

Figure 7.6

1 *Music*
Signature tune (15 seconds)
Fade down to

2 *Presenter 1*
Welcome to Palmer's Radio – your very own college radio station – and I'm Dan, your Friday host. Today, we are going to look at how to survive university without sinking under a mountain of debt, drugs and debauchery! We've asked some ex-Palmer's students to reveal their very own experiences of life at university – is it all as good as it's cracked up to be?

But first its over to Karen who's out and about talking to you about what you think university life is like.

Fade out music

3 Background of Common Room (3 seconds)

4 Presenter 2
Hi everyone, I'm here in the Blue Room to get some of your opinions about university life ...

Well, that's enough of what you think university might be like. Let's now hear from some students who have found out firsthand since leaving Palmer's.

Cue sheet

Programme:	Friday Lunchtime Show
Subject:	Life at university
Presenter:	Karen
Duration:	3-4 minutes
Cue:	Hi everyone, I'm here in the Blue Room to get some of your opinions about university life ... Well, that's enough of what you think university might be like. Let's now hear from some students who have found out firsthand since leaving Palmer's.
In:	Music fade out/background noise of Blue Room
Out:	As above

Figure 7.7

VIDEO

Advantages

The most obvious appeal of video is that it is capable of making a strong impact. We live in an age where the moving image is the most popular (and powerful) media form. Compared to the printed image, word or sound, video has the advantage of being able to combine all three elements when communicating with the audience. It also offers the most potential for creativity, both in the recording and editing phases.

Considerations

In production work, a storyboard (see the example on page 27) is nearly always essential. This should take account of the need for:

- **structure** having a sequence that allows the audience to follow the narrative easily;
- **variety of shots** providing a range of perspectives and framings (long shot to close up);
- **sound** whether this is to be natural or dubbed on later;
- **shooting schedule** indicating clearly where and when the recording will take place.

Production ideas

- *Music sound tracks*
  This kind of sound involves a simple dubbing exercise in which different musical extracts are dubbed on to a pre-recorded video sequence. Music affects the meaning of an image. Music can be added with the intention of creating suspense, romance, humour or sadness.

- *Short promo*
  A promo is a short (30 seconds–1 minute) video that 'advertises' or 'sells' a particular product or service. In the case of a school or college, it could be produced to promote the whole institution (to parents of prospective students) or a part of it such as the sporting facilities or library. The discipline required is that of constructing the video in a way that conveys a very positive image or 'message' to the target audience.

- *Suspense*
  This involves a short sequence of 20–30 shots that help to build towards a climax that leaves the audience in suspense. Techniques for achieving suspense include:

  - using closer and closer shots;
  - presenting something that is mysterious, such as a shadowy figure;
  - the audience knowing something the character doesn't;
  - the audience anticipating what will happen next;
  - using appropriate music and sound effects.

Video assignment

TASK

To design a storyboard (see Figure 7.9) for the title sequence of a new television police series.

Production process

1 Examine at least two examples of title sequences from the genre to identify typical conventions used in constructing such sequences.

2 Devise a *new* series that you are going to design your title sequence storyboard for. You will need to have a clear idea of the setting, main characters and their relationships, the kind of plot lines and action occurring in an episode, scheduling and, of course, the series' title!

3 Construct a storyboard for the title sequence. It should contain detailed visual information (concerning camerawork, framing, lighting, and so on) and accompanying music (it would help to supply a tape if the music already exists). The maximum number of shots is 16.

4 Provide an accompanying explanatory guide as to what the aims of the title sequence are and why the specific shots and music have been selected.

Figure 7.8

STORYBOARD SHEET

SHOT No.	SKETCH	VISUAL (subject and low shot-framing, camera movement, etc)	SOUND (dialogue, music sound effects)	TIME

Figure 7.9

Advantages

Now that computers are widely available in schools and colleges, students are able to design and 'publish' print media products such as newspapers and magazines using desktop publishing (DTP) software – Microsoft Publisher or Quark Xpress (the current industry standard), for example. A scanner for converting printed images into digital files that can be inserted into text files on a computer is all that is needed to complete the package. It is still possible to use 'cut and paste' techniques as a 'low-tech' solution, but it is certainly exciting to be able to come close to professional standards of production as is possible using DTP.

Newspapers and magazines are particularly effective in targeting specific audiences. Any interest can be catered for and the content written and designed to meet the needs of its readers. From the production point of view, the product can be easily altered on screen and there is scope to be experimental. Indeed, the material can be developed continually in response to feedback from would-be readers.

For the most ambitious, there is now the opportunity to really embrace new technology by creating a homepage on the Internet.

Considerations

The main factors to take into account when producing print media materials are the:

- **Target readers**
  everything needs to be tailored to suit their needs if the finished product is to be attractive to them;

- **Language**
  the way the product 'talks' to its readers (the mode of address) – the choice of vocabulary, use of technical terms and so on;

- **Design**
  how the pages are laid out, the choice of typeface (font), the use of colour and other visual details;

- **Image/text**
  the desired balance between images and written text on each page.

Production ideas

- **Newspaper's front page**
  There are national and local, broadsheet and tabloid newspapers. If you want to construct your own, stories can either be made up, or better still, adapted from a news supply (such as 24-hour TV or radio news channels, on-line newspaper web pages). A front page should include:
  - a **mast head** title – the title of the paper;
  - a **banner** headline ('splash') – headline in large print for the main story;
  - the **lead** story – the main story;
  - two or three secondary headlines and stories;
  - one or two pictures with captions.

Figure 7.10

- **Double-page magazine feature**

  This kind of article is on a topic that fits the identity of the magazine it appears in. The key points to remember here are to assume good, well-researched writing and effective design. Essential features of good design include:

  – clear signposting by means of different headlines, type sizes and positioning of text;
  – a distinctive style or character, achieved by careful use of of design features, such as typefaces;
  – a look that suits the subject of the feature and the magazine.

  The starting point for any production work is a **page plan** (see Figure 7.10).

- **A website**

  As with all print media, there needs to be a clear justification for creating such a site – that is, there needs to be a potential Internet audience. Serving a specialist interest, whether it be local, national or even global, is the most frequent motivation. Identifying the best features of other comparable websites is a good way to start. It is then a case of creating a front, or **homepage**, adding extra pages and creating links between pages by means of easily identified clickable 'hotspots'. The overall aim is to allow the user to navigate easily through the site in search of information.

  To create a webpage, it is helpful to have web design software, such as WYSIWYG (what you see is what you get) or Microsoft Frontpage. However, it is possible to create a simple page using a HTML edit program, which comes with Netscape or Microsoft browsers. The Internet itself has websites devoted to helping people create their own websites. Examples include www.webmonkey and web developer.

  Eventually, your own website could be added to the Internet free of charge, providing you get permission from your Internet service provider. (Remember to ensure that you have not included any images for which you need to seek permission to use).

Print assignment

TASK

To create the front cover for the first edition of a new magazine.

Production process

1 decide on the subject matter of the magazine, how it will be treated (if it will be serious, light-hearted, traditional, innovative);

2 identify your target audience (age, class, lifestyle);

3 examine any similar magazines already on the market – look at how their front covers have been designed – and see how (if at all) they influence your ideas;

4 construct the front cover, paying particular attention to:
  - the title (and possibly include a magazine 'motto');
  - dominant images(s);
  - the coverlines, including the main feature;
  - typefaces;
  - colour;
  - artwork;
  - layout;

NB: before using a computer, create a rough 'mock-up' of the cover in which you sketch in the main features;

5 obtain some critical feedback from a small sample of your target audience and include this within a short written account in which you explain the thinking behind your design and evaluate the strengths and weaknesses of the front page you have designed.

INDEX

ACKNOWLEDGEMENTS

We are grateful to the following for permission to reproduce copyright photographs and material:

AOL/Time Warner for page 68; Aardman Animations for page 4 (still from *The Wrong Trousers* ©1993 Wallace and Gromit Ltd, a member of the Aardman Animations group of companies); Age Concern for page 95; Aiwa for page 74 (top right); Attic Futura for page 29 (the article 'Blast from the past' from Inside Soap Magazine, 23/7/99); Aquarius Picture Library for page 147; Audi UK for page 49 (bottom right); BBC for page 4 (Hancock), 32, 48, 70 (top right and bottom right), 86, 89, 109 (top left), 136 (bottom), 142, 145; BBC Broadcasting Research for page 60 (extract from Eastenders: The Research Contribution (BBC Audience Research Findings 1986)); BBC Enterprises for page 59 (Don Smith/front cover of Radio Times); Barnardo's for page 92 (top right); Benetton for page 49 (top right), 50; Big! Magazine for page 4 (front cover); Blackwell Publishers for page 7 (extract from *The British Press and Broadcasting Since 1945* by C. Seymour-Ure); Bliss for page 72 (top); British Board of Film Classification for page 46 (bottom); Broadcast for page 35 (top right), 41, 65 (bottom right); Broadcasters Audience Research Board for page 111 (bottom right), 139; Buxton Spring for page 22 (top); J Allan Cash Ltd for page 91 (bottom right); Andy Catlin for page 106; Channel Four Television for page 46 (top), 96, 148; Classic FM for page 4 (logo); Collections for page 16 (top right); The Committe of Advertising Practice for extract from alcoholic drinks section of British Codes of Advertising page 51 – full codees are available to download from either http://www.cap.org.uk or http://www.asa.org.uk; Curtis Management Group on behalf of the James Dean Foundation for page 94 (bottom); The Daily Star for page 4 (front cover), 103 (front cover); The Daily Telegraph for page 103 (front cover); EMAP for page 40 (article *Tricks of the Trade* in Broadcast, 21/1/99) and page 32 (extract from Broadcast 21/6/98); Eidos/Core Design for page 8, 9, 10 (Lara Croft); Express Newspapers for page 84 (bottom), 85 (top), 88 (bottom), 103 (front cover), 132 (bottom right); Financial Times for page 103 (front cover); Front Magazine for page 79 (top right); Granada Television for page 34; Kenneth Green Associates for page 71 (top); The Guardian News Service for page 33, 40 (Best Sellers list), 88, 53, 63 (top), 67, 85 (bottom), 103 (front cover); Hal Leonard Corporation for page 27 (storyboard from *How to Shoot Better Video* by R. Hirschman and R. Proctor); Haymarket Campaign Publications Ltd for page 14 (bottom), 118; David Hoffman for page 14 (top); IBM for page 82 (top); IPC Magazines for page 25-26; The Independent for page 16 (top left and middle left), 18, 43 (the author Nicholas Barber for an extract from the article 'Fresh from Mr Spice – 4/4/99 and photos), 58, 76 ('Game, Chest and Match' from the article 'More Balls please!' by Ingrid Kennedy in The Independent on Sunday, 27/6/99), 81, 103 (front cover); Inside Soap Magazine for page 29 (photo), 35 (middle left); ITC for page 47; Just 17 for page 130 (top left); Kerrang! Magazine for page 107 (top right); The Kobal Collection for page 20, 97 (top right and bottom), 109 (top middle); LWT for page 4 (Logo); Later Magazine for page 121 (top left and bottom left); Lee Jeans for page 83; Little Brown & Company for page 36 (extract from *Hollywood Dream Factory*), 44; Lucasfilm Ltd TM & ©Lucasfilm Ltd (LFC); Lyons Tetley Ltd for page 4 (advert); MGM for page 4 (Clint Eastwood); MCA Publishing for page 24; Ewan McNaughton Associates for page 133 (Eddie Mulholland/bottom); MacMillan Press for page 38 (top right); Marie Claire for page 130 (bottom right); Match for page 72 (bottom); Max Magazine for page 129 (bottom right); Me Company for page 4 (Shaman CD cover "Boss Drum); Minx Magazine for page 121 (top right and bottom right); Mirror Syndication for page 37 (front cover), 54 (bottom), 93, 103 (front cover); Moulinex Swan Holdings Ltd for page 79 (bottom right); NEFF for page 79 (bottom left); National Magazine Company Ltd for page 92 (bottom); National Viewers and Listeners Association for page 140; Nescafe for page 22 (bottom); News Corporation Ltd for page 42 (an extract from News Corporation Annual Report 1999); News Group Newspapers Ltd for page 17, 54 (top), 75, 84 (top), 103 (front cover); News International Syndication for page 76 (for the article 'Korn's in good shape' by Steven Howard in The Sun – 22/6/99 © News International Newspapers Ltd, 1999); Nike for page 127; The Observor for page 16 (bottom right), 31; Pan MacMillan Ltd for page 27 (top); Paramount Pictures for page 98; Pearson Television for page 21, 70 (bottom left), 108, 109 (top right); Peugeot for page 13; Pilkington plc for page 74 (top left); Plain Dealer Publishing Company for page 100; Playstation for page 4 (Grand Theft Auto), 128; Polygram International Music Publishing

Ltd for page 23 (song lyrics of *Always* by Bon Jovi); Pride for page 131 (bottom right); RAJAR for page 113; Radio Times for page 30, 102 (from Eastenders article by Tony Holland, illustrated by Tony Draper, photos by Don Smith, 16-22/285), 110 (top right), 125; Rex Features Ltd for page 94 (top); Reuters Stills Library for page 91 (bottom left); Ronald Grant Film Library for pages 12 and 28; Scope Features for page 70 (top left); Sight and Sound/British Film Institute for an extract from 'The ScheduleSky TV for page 4 (Bart Simpson); Solo Syndication/IPC Magazines for page 37 (front cover), 77, 78, 88 (bottom right), 103 (front cover); Spotlight Publications for page 35 (bottom left), 104, 120; Sunrise Radio Ltd for page 90; TV Times for page 80, 85 (middle), 126; Take a Break for page 131 (top left); Time Out for page 63 (bottom); Times Newspapers for page 103 (front cover), 111 (cartoon by Peter Schrank ©Times Supplements Ltd, 1986/top left), 132 (Peter Brookes/middle); Twentieth Century Fox for page 97 (top), 99 (top); VSW Publications for page 107 (bottom right); Virgin Interactive for page 4 (Robocop & Terminator games); Viz for page 4 (logo); The Voice for page 88 (top right); James Wood Associates for page 49 (bottom left); Woolwich Building Society for page 122; Yorkshire Television Stills Library for page 110 (top left); Zine Magazine for page 62.

We have been unable to trace the copyright holders of the following material and would appreciate any information, which would enable us to do so:

Pages 4 (David Bowie CD cover, Handbag.com logo, Radio 1 FM van), 6, 14 (middle), 15 (graffiti adverts), 16 (middle right), 19, 36 (star power list), 38 (newspaper circulation chart), 39 (advertising costs chart), 45, 51, 52, 55, 64, 66, 71 (bottom), 73, 74 (bottom left), 82 (bottom), 87, 91 (top right), 107 (middle left and bottom left), 112, 114, 115, 116, 117, 119, 123, 129 (top left), 133 (middle), 134, 135, 137, 138, 141, 147.

Although every effort has been made to trace the owners of copyright material, in a few cases this has proved impossible and we take this opportunity to offer our apologies to any copyright holders whose rights may have been unwittingly infringed.